Wildcats of Finance

Lowdown on Hedge Funds and Suchlike

for

Investors and Policymakers

Steven H. Kim

MintKit Press

MintKit.com

Copyright © 2011 by *Steven H. Kim*

Contents

Preface

In recent decades, hedge funds have played a growing role in causing or aggravating blowups in the capital markets as well as the banking system. The biggest bombshell thus far was the crisis of 2008, which ended up crippling the financial system along with the real economy.

As the debacle played out, trillions of dollars went up in smoke in each of the major stock markets of the world. Another turnout was the destruction of millions of jobs and the squelch of trillions of dollars by way of lost output in every major country.

The carnage round the globe led to widespread calls by an incensed populace for the government to step in and rein in the horde of hedge funds that had led the charge in the run-up to the meltdown. The proponents of reform set their sights on wildcats ranging from boutique funds standing on their own to coddled groups ensconced within commercial banks.

The pivotal role of the risk mongers in stoking and inflaming blowups in the marketplace gave rise to a flurry of fiats aimed at hedge funds of all stripes. Amid the hubbub, politicians responded in their usual fashion by drumming up fetters meant to tone down the orgies of speculation in the marketplace.

On a positive note, the aims of the policymakers surely lay in the right direction. No sane person would argue against measures to safeguard the welfare of the investing public as well as the health of the global economy.

If the past is prologue, though, the pile of cuffs cobbled together by the lawmakers merely serves to muck up the machinery of the financial system. In that case, the main impact of the legislation is an upsurge of bureaucracy and busywork in the marketplace in tandem with a cutback of productivity and prosperity in the economy at large.

To spotlight the crux of the problem, we can compare the situation to the task of stamping out wildfires in a forest. The knee-jerk response to a financial crisis is akin to forcing every camper in a forest to keep a detailed record of their activities, and to validate each entry by obtaining a seal of compliance from a licensed inspector.

On the other hand, a shortage of make-work was not the cause of the firestorms in the first place. As a result, piling on the paperwork will merely serve to degrade the experience of the great outdoors for every camper without having any material effect on the root of the problem.

For this reason, a slew of red tape will have scant impact on the frequency or severity of wildfires. On the contrary, a false sense of security may well prompt the campers to pay less attention to the activities that really matter in stoking a blaze: lighting bonfires, smoking cigarettes, dumping flammables, and other acts of similar ilk.

Moving closer to home, the same type of bungling cropped up after the binge of speculation and fraud that beset the stock market during the Internet craze of the 1990s. The mound of regulations whipped up in the aftermath of the blowout merely ended up imposing a heavy burden on public companies.

The inevitable outturn was to throttle productivity in every segment of the financial forum as well as the real economy. One direct impact was the cutdown of earnings for millions of shareholders standing behind the companies listed on the stock exchange.

Another noxious outcome was an uptick in the cost of products for all types of consumers. Since the shackled vendors had to recoup the billions of dollars frittered away in witless paperwork every year, their obvious recourse was to pay for the waste by hiking the prices charged to their customers.

Worst of all, though, the pile of legislation was unable to prevent the next bubble that began to flare up within a couple of years. The newborn craze led to a bubble in real estate and related assets, followed in due course by the blowup of 2008. As things turned out, the knock-on crisis caused far more damage than the earlier bust due to the Internet bash.

In fact, the latest bombshell turned into the biggest blowup of the financial sector since the 1930s. Another turnout was the worst recession in the global economy since the Second World War.

Needless to say – but surely worth saying – the mass of regulations cooked up during the first few years of the millennium failed to meet its objectives. On the contrary, the mound of ill-conceived yokes merely served to exacerbate the follow-on flap.

For one thing, the chains on public companies caused them to dissipate a lot of time, money and energy on revamping their procedures and documenting their activities. The resources expended could have been put to much better use by expanding the scope of operations or improving the level of productivity.

The huge waste of effort doubtless played a crucial role in the anemic recovery in the business sector along with the overall economy. As a result, the central bank had to keep interest rates at abnormally low levels for years on end in a grim attempt to nudge up the pace of economic activity.

Cutting down the basic rate of interest is accomplished by unleashing a gush of money into the financial system. Given the deluge of liquidity sloshing around the marketplace, it was only a matter of time before a raft of assets in the financial forum as well as the real economy would bubble up and boil over.

In this frothy setting, a gaggle of gamesters on Wall Street and Main Street joined hands to cook up the shakiest of schemes. The piddly rates of interest provided the backdrop for churning out a torrent of loans to borrowers regardless of their credit ratings. The torrent of debt included scads of mortgages issued to applicants with little or no ability to keep up with the installment payments in the years to follow.

The loans pumped out were then sold by the banksters to a bunch of promoters. The hucksters in turn packaged the hunks of debt into a welter of securities for sale to the investing public.

In this way, the mountain of regulations stamped out in the wake of the Internet madness failed to serve its mission with great distinction. The objective of the busywork was to stamp out deceptive marketing and mindless speculation. The outcome was precisely the opposite.

The heart of the problem lay in the muff of dealing with the symptoms rather than the causes of the malaise. Not surprisingly, the heap of legislation had no effect on the disease itself. For this reason, the main impact of the sanctions was to destroy wealth year after year by imposing gobs of busywork on hapless firms in every industry.

In a similar way, the heap of laws cranked out in 2009 and thereafter would at best treat a few of the byproducts rather than root out the germs of the ailment. If any diktats are to fulfill their goals, though, the real causes need to be addressed.

To this end, sweeping changes in regulation are required in order to counter the threat from hedge funds armed with weapons of mass mayhem. As a starting point for sorting out the muddle, a basic goal of this book is to uncover the real sources of sickness in the marketplace. A related task is to present a wholesome set of remedies designed to wipe out the pandemic by the roots.

Crux of the Malady

To sum up, hedge funds have played a growing role in causing or abetting blowups in the capital markets as well as banking institutions. The biggest blowup thus far was the crisis of 2008, which ended up wrecking the financial system and trashing the larger economy to boot.

The catastrophe obliterated trillions of dollars from each of the major stock markets of the world. Another feat was to destroy millions of jobs in scores of countries and to trash trillions of dollars by way of lost output in the global economy.

The carnage in the marketplace led to enraged calls amongst the general public for the government to step in and rein in the ringleaders in the form of hedge funds. The targets in the crosshairs ranged from boutique funds standing on their own to coddled groups nestled within mercantile banks.

In response to the clangor, policymakers scampered around for easy ways to prevent such flaps in the future. Sadly, though, the pat answers they pounced on were destined to hobble the financial markets while doing little or nothing to eradicate the threats for real. As is their wont, the pols took the facile route by fiddling with the syndrome on the periphery instead of stamping out the disease at the epicenter.

The pile of regulations churned out can only gum up the financial markets without clearing away the deep-seated ills. At its core, the stumper lies in the lopsided matchup of reward and penalty in the vale of hedge funds. A second, and related, bogey is the batty scheme of handing out princely bonuses in return for sham performance amongst the so-called professionals in the financial sector as well as the real economy.

In addition, the hazards are compounded by the ease of taking up loony amounts of leverage. One form of unbridled risk lies in the instruments of mass carnage known as financial derivatives. Another type of outsized risk stems from the mounds of leverage provided through loans from commercial banks.

Under the current system of payoffs, the operators of hedge funds walk off with a hefty chunk the booty in the wake of a profitable spree. In the aftermath of a disastrous spell, however, the stewards merely pass on the cost of the failure to the investors, shareholders and other external parties.

Under this arrangement, the punters have nothing to lose by taking on boundless amounts of risk. The inevitable result is to pummel the assets under management and pulverize the capital entrusted to them.

A careful survey of the public record reveals that the practice in the hedge fund game does in fact conform to the logic of the setup. The upshot is to whack the investors and other stakeholders when the bets go sour, as they always do at some point.

In an affront to fairness as well as prudence, the payoff reaped by the operators tends to swell with the level of risk – regardless of the final fate of the portfolio or the average performance prior to the meltdown. On the other hand, the loss to the outsiders of course increases with the magnitude of the risk.

The intrinsic flaws in the market reach well beyond the fortunes of the operators and their patrons. Sadly, the chains of bondage among the bettors, creditors and investors can and do lead at times to a blowup of the entire system of finance and banking as well as the meshwork of production and consumption.

Amid the muddle and the turmoil, the purpose of this guidebook is to shed light on a murky field where illusion and hokum run amok. The subjects in hand range from the lot of the operator and the investor to the fate of the market and the economy.

The topics in focus include the following items.

- How the true performance of hedge funds remains hidden from view of the investing public.
- Why the operators of shadowy pools go out on a limb to pursue risky bets.
- How the statistics of the marketplace reveal only the tip of the iceberg, the bulk of which remains under water.
- Why the interests of the operators are opposed to those of the investors.
- How the managers of pooled accounts can boost their profits by delivering worse results for their customers.
- Why wildcat groups within traditional firms are as dangerous as boutique funds.
- How the top tier of heavyweights – whose trading records are available for inspection – underperforms inert cash under the mattress in terms of gross returns, let alone net payoffs, after adjusting for errors due to biased sampling.
- How the reality belies the illusion of performance even amongst the fabled legends of hedge funds, for reasons ranging from faulty classification and selective amnesia to foul play and sudden death.
- Why hedge funds in the aggregate destroy wealth for their customers as well as innocent bystanders in the financial forum as well as the real economy.
- How the destruction of wealth occurs at the microlevel of the individual investor as well as the macrolevel of the financial markets and the real economy.
- Why robotic agents – also known as *algorithmic traders* or simply as *algos* – are often confused with hedge funds.
- How the algos siphon off billions of dollars a year from ordinary investors in each of the major markets round the world.
- How the algos slash the payoff and hoist the risk for the investing public in a chronic and draining fashion, while

hedge funds do likewise in an acute and catastrophic way; in other words, hack by a zillion cuts as opposed to death in one fell stroke.

- Why the pat responses of policymakers serve only to paper over the symptoms rather than root out the ailments.
- How the economic liability of hedge funds can be turned into a social asset.
- Why the monster crash of 2008 and the Great Recession in its wake will show up repeatedly in the future, and wreak devastation on a greater scale, unless proper safeguards are put in place beforehand.

In short, the goal of this book is to give the lowdown on the biggest threats in the financial forum as well as the tangible economy. To this end, a primal task is to uncover the true cause and full scope of the malaise without pulling any punches. In this light, the crucial factors run the gamut from motive forces to hidden impacts.

Another objective is to survey the obstacles to reform in a candid way and to present a trenchant set of remedies to set things right. The malaise in the financial forum and the real economy has to be tackled in an incisive and thorough fashion in order to defang the bugbear with dispatch.

A hallmark of the volume is a cogent set of measures designed to uproot the malady at the source instead of puttering round the edges. Unlike the schemes concocted to date by harried lawmakers in a hurry, the object of the treatment is to cure the disease rather than merely mask the syndrome.

The main audience for the book consists of active investors and earnest policymakers. Other types of readers range from concerned professionals in the financial community to thoughtful observers in all walks of life.

The financial crisis of 2008, along with its aftermath, has underscored the fact that the fortunes of Wall Street and Main Street are tightly intertwined. Given the tie-up between the financial forum and the real economy, the contents of this book are in fact relevant not only to serious investors in the marketplace but to casual observers standing on the sidelines.

From a larger stance, consumers and producers of all stripes have a vested interest in the goings-on in the financial bazaar whether they realize it or not. For this reason, everyone ought to care about the stumper to a greater or lesser degree, and to spare a thought for the clutch of issues examined within these pages.

— *S.K.*

Chapter 1

Invisible Threat

Like a swarm of icebergs, the bulk of hedge funds lurks out of sight. The lack of visibility, along with the danger it entails, is a hallmark of individual outfits as well as the entire throng.

Veiled from public view, it's the hidden mass that inflicts most of the damage to investors and other stakeholders. Yet the frequency and severity of meltdowns are poorly understood by the financial community as well as the general public.

From a different angle, the setup is similar to a jaunt on a flimsy boat in the stormy seas of finance. When the customers sign up for a fling on these dinghies, little do they know that a shipwreck is the usual fate in the realm of hedge funds.

Without realizing it, the patrons in effect agree to pay the operators a fat bonus depending on the level of excitement. The rougher the ride, the bigger the reward.

Moreover, the clients agree that only the crew in charge will be entitled to life belts in case of a mishap at sea. When the craft hits a wall of ice and sinks, the entire throng of passengers goes down with the wreckage while the stewards flee the scene without a scratch or blotch.

As the folly of the arrangement finally dawns on the trippers, it's of course far too late to escape the dunking. When a vessel breaks down and goes under, the riders have to consider themselves lucky if they lose only their shirts and get to keep their pants.

With the passage of time, the victims of the drubbing are apt to get over the shock and regain their composure. Even at that stage, though, the majority will fail to grasp the true nature of the harrowing experience they just endured.

For the most part, the hapless patrons will chalk up the fiasco to a stroke of bad luck. In the process, the clients will get their cue from the operators, whose standard reaction is to shrug off the debacle as a plain fluke.

According to the flip response from the stewards, no one could have foreseen the catastrophe. After all, the future is unknown and unknowable – right?

If truth be told, though, an argument of this sort is a model of sophistry where hedge funds are concerned. The claim is akin to careening down a road at high speed in a fog, then calling the resulting accident a bolt out of the blue.

Granted, the upset on the road was unintended. Moreover, the details of the crackup could not have been foreseen.

Despite the iffy factors at work, though, the smashup was a foregone conclusion just the same. The only real question was the way in which the joy ride would come to a sudden and jarring end. The details might differ from one romp to another, but the sorry outcome is preordained.

In racing down the highway at full throttle, the best that can be hoped for is a gradual slowdown as the vehicle veers off the road and plows into a field. The corresponding outcome in the land of hedge funds is a portfolio that slowly shrinks in value, thus giving the patrons enough time to escape with the remnants of their withered assets.

Sadly, though, the usual turnout is far more devastating. All too often, the finale takes the form of a crash and burn, leaving the investors with little or nothing left to salvage.

In short, the customers who sign up for a joy ride are largely unaware of the wipeout looming on the horizon. To top it all off, the bombshell does not leave them any wiser after the fact. Rather, the bulk of the casualties come to believe that their experience was a freak exception rather than the general rule.

Chapter 2

False Identity

In a number of ways, the hedge fund – also known in some circles as a *hedgie* – is a feral as well as frail creature. Sadly for the investing public, though, the image of the breed is entirely at odds with the reality.

In the usual parlance of the financial world, or even in everyday life, a "hedge" is a protective scheme or a defensive move whose function is to limit the scope of risk. In fact, one popular dictionary defines a hedge as "an act or means of preventing complete loss" in the case of a bet or an investment, by making a countermove in order to offset the risk at hand. Put another way, the role of a hedge is to fend off a devastating loss.

By contrast, the standard practice in the hedge fund game is to jack up the risk in the hope of hitting the jackpot. In fact, the operators draw in their clients through the claim – whether express or implied – that the scheme can snag a windfall with piffling risk.

Behind the scenes, though, the actions taken by the hustlers belie the pledges they make. In many cases, the exposure to risk is wholly deliberate.

An exemplar involves a speculator that takes up an overstretched position using a financial derivative. For instance, the punter might buy a bunch of futures contracts on gold bullion in order to place a bigger bet than they could by procuring the metal itself.

In other cases, the precarious nature of a levered bet stems from a fond hope coupled with a defective grasp of the marketplace. An example involves a "hedger" who buys a futures contract on silver and sells a comparable stake on gold. The hedged position would bag a profit if the change in the silver contract were to exceed that for gold.

On any given day, the price of the two metals can move independently of each other. Over the long term, though, silver tends to follow the lead set by gold.

Furthermore, the relative change in price for the white metal tends to be larger than that for its golden sibling. Due to the divergence in prices, the purchase of silver coupled with the sale of gold is prone to show a net profit when the entire market for precious metals happens to enjoy an upswing.

Naturally, the same process works in reverse during a downtrend. More precisely, the two-pronged gambit is wont to show a loss when the market for precious metals breaks down.

The purpose of a futures contract is to amplify the change in price for a target asset while the trader puts up only a small deposit to serve as collateral for the wager. For this reason, the purchase or sale of the financial instrument exposes the punter to greater risk in comparison to a direct bet on the metal itself.

In line with earlier remarks, both gold and silver can thrash wildly from one day to the next, or even in the blink of an eye. As a result, a levered play – whether hedged or not – can wipe out a trading account in a flash. In fact, a punter could lose everything faster than they can drop their jaws or pull out their hair while screeching "No, no, nooooo!"

For this reason, the setup with futures contracts happens to be aggressive rather than defensive. In other words, the two-part gambit – of buying silver and selling gold – is a hedge in a literal sense, but not in a meaningful way. On the contrary, a hedged ploy using levered tools is apt to be far more hazardous than an unhedged scheme which steers clear of any kind of gearing.

To recap, the bettor in the futures market did set up a hedged position in a literal sense. On the other hand, the plunger went out on a limb by taking up the leverage furnished by futures contracts.

The purpose of a levered gambit is to amplify the impact of price changes by putting up only a pittance at the outset. The small deposit serves as the collateral, also known in the financial bazaar as the *margin* for the position.

The express function of each contract is to magnify the shift in price whenever the market swells or swoons. In other words, the crankup of risk is an integral aspect of a levered position.

Unfortunately, an updraft in the financial forum is always followed by a downstroke sooner or later. For this reason, the surge of profits on the upswing turns into a gush of losses on the downleg.

High Risk and Low Gain

Due to the tumult in the marketplace, along with the fondness for leverage, hedge funds of all breeds bite the dust in droves. Even the ablest players have a way of going out of business at the rate of one-half within a few years of their rollout.

Going Bust en Masse

Most of the heavyweights in the hedge fund game set up their vehicles as offshore pools, far from the watchful eyes of the regulators located in major countries. Within this group of players, around 20% of the outfits go kaput every year.[1]

Given the high rate of mortality, it's no surprise that most of the funds on record have stunted histories. At first glance, an attrition rate of one-fifth of the entrants every year may not sound so hairy to some folks.

On the other hand, a takedown at that clip means that the half-life of the hedgies is 3.1 years. In other words, a pool chosen at random will have roughly even odds of dying off in about three years.

Frightful as it is, the span of three years could well be a generous estimate of the longevity, or lack of such. According to a different study, the half-life of hedge funds was *less* than 2.5 years.[2]

At the latter rate of demise, three-quarters of the outfits would bite the dust within half a decade. In this parlous setting, the patrons who hand over their money can rest assured that most of them will end up in tears within a few short years.

Rueful Returns of the Survivors

The alarming rate of mortality in the hedge fund game is bad enough. On the other hand, the performance of the survivors is nothing to write home about, either.

The eye-opening results come from a medley of impartial studies. The occasional reports based on rigorous research happen to represent a refreshing counterweight to the usual claims resulting from slapdash compilations of whatever data happen to be close to hand.

The conclusions from the incisive studies are not flattering, to say the least. According to the telling probes, the top tier of hedge funds turns in *gross* profits that on average trail behind those of mutual funds.

For their part, mutual funds have a long history of lagging the benchmarks of the market. As a result, investors in general get the short end of the stick when they hand their money over to the managed pools.

Sadly, the end result is even worse in the hedge fund game: the net payout to the investors falls far short of the average gain eked out by mutual funds. There are several reasons for the gap in performance.

To begin with, hedge funds impose a fixed fee based on the total value of the assets under management regardless of the performance of the portfolio. The maintenance charge usually amounts to some 2% of the assets each year. For certain cases, however, the levy can balloon to 5% per annum.

In addition, the custodians take a cut of the winnings each time the portfolio happens to turn in a profit. As a rule, the fees range from 20 to 50 percent of the profits; but in some cases the cutout may be lower or higher than the standard range.

On the flip side, though, the operators pay no penalty when the portfolio declines in value. Rather, the investors get to foot the whole bill in case of a flop.

A Losing Game

Given the high risk and low payout on offer, the hedge fund game is clearly a losing proposition for the clients. In fact, the investing public could earn more profits with less risk by turning to vehicles which are far more robust as well as transparent. A fine example of the latter is an index fund whose return is geared to the performance of a market benchmark.

Given this backdrop, the setup in the hedge fund game is a sweet deal for the operators but a sour play for their customers. In that case, why do so many investors hanker after such pools?

The only plausible answer is that the mass of investors do not realize what they're getting into. To begin with, the mantle of secrecy surrounding the den of hedge funds is not conducive to making clear-headed decisions.

Moreover, the usual statistics of the marketplace have a raft of shortcomings. Yet the numbers are reported at face value by a horde of service providers, industry boosters, and financial media. In this blustery climate, the raw numbers project an image of hedge funds which belies the reality.

Hidden Bogeys

Despite the perils of hedge funds, the majority of investors have scant idea of the dangers in store. The entire domain is shrouded in a mantle of smog and streaked with a touch of mystique.

For starters, the allure of hedge funds oozes in part from an air of exclusivity. Due to official regulations, the outfits are supposed to cater only to moneyed investors.

Another source of fatal attraction lies in the tantalizing whispers of great riches that hover on the grapevine. As it happens, the vast majority of washouts in the hedge fund game are buried quietly. Moreover, the few deadbeats that crop up on the rumor mill are generally dismissed as the forgettable duds that they are.

By contrast, the rare feats of triumph in the field are feted with great fanfare by the mass media and the general public. Moreover, the tales of success are celebrated and recounted for years or even decades on end.

What the clients of hedge funds do not realize is that they are in effect simply buying tickets to an ornate lottery. Sadly, the patrons see only part of the picture and remain blissfully unaware of the dirty laundry kept out of view.

Bias in the Media

A simple way to explain the bias in the financial press is to examine a parallel with other forms of betting. Suppose that the mass media were to devote an inordinate amount of time to the winners of the local casino or state lottery. Meanwhile, the newscasts conveniently fail to describe the plight of the mass of bettors who end up with nothing.

In that case, a lot of viewers would sit up in their chairs and take a shine to gambling. For this to happen, all that's required is to serve up a distorted picture of the sweepstakes.

To kindle interest in the subject, the operators of the games would talk up the gleeful cases of lucky souls who hit the jackpot. By contrast, the hucksters would maintain a code of silence concerning the losers and brush aside any talk of casualties in the field.

In addition, the reporters on the sidelines would focus on the gains to be snagged by the bettors while giving short shrift to the losses. By the same token, the mass media would declare a moratorium – whether explicitly or tacitly – on the deluge of wipeouts suffered by the vast majority of players.

Under these conditions, the outcome would be similar to the near-total blackout on rubouts in the hedge fund game. In that case, the general public could not help but get the impression that just about anyone can reap a fortune by playing the sweepstakes, whether in the form of public raffles, casino games, or hedge funds.

To be fair, the mass media does bring up the subject of mishaps once in a blue moon. A case in point was a passing nod to the wholesale breakdown of hedge funds during the financial crisis of 2008.

Even here, though, the extent of the carnage was scarcely mentioned. Instead, the crackup of the hedgies en masse was glossed over and presented for the most part as if the flops were rare and minor events.

Another turnout of the financial crisis was the breakdown of a host of reckless firms in areas ranging from investment banking to commercial insurance. Granted, some of the crackups were far too big for anyone to ignore. As a result, there was little choice for the mass media but to report on the behemoths that blew up with a loud bang.

On the other hand, there was apparently no need to pay much heed to the swarm of minnows smashed to bits in the shoals of the hedge fund game. Based on the skimpy reports coming across the news wires, the audience would get the impression that the mass extermination of the shrimps was merely a sideshow amid the occasional rubout of the whales.

Unhappily, though, the truth was very different: hedge funds of all breeds took center stage in causing the fiasco and exacerbating the aftershock. Not surprisingly, the punters also went belly up in droves. The mass extermination of the hedgies, along with the larger conflagration in the marketplace, were the unavoidable turnouts of the inflated role of the bettors in the marketplace.

Reality May be Tragic but not Gripping

In line with earlier remarks, the mass media contributed to the malaise – however innocently – by harping on the glitter of hedge funds while giving short shrift to the tawdry side. It was not even a matter of giving equal time to both the upside and the downside.

If the members of the press were to sketch out a fair and accurate picture, they would have had to present scores of losers for every winner. While the media did not create the problems in the hedge fund game, but they did contribute to the muddle by presenting a misleading picture of the domain.

Going forward, the members of the press could choose instead to play a helpful role for the investing public. An example in this vein is to guard against trotting out sham data at face value. If any such figures are to be aired, the presentation should be accompanied by a clear explanation that the statistics happen to spring from highly biased samples.

In the interest of clarity and probity, the media ought to point out that the occasional feats of success are more than negated by a slew of flops. The situation in the hedge fund game is somewhat akin to the throng of hopefuls that flock to Hollywood. Every actor who rises to stardom is matched by a cast of thousands who fail to fulfill their goals.

On the other hand, the good folks in the media cannot be expected to do more than their fare share in setting the record straight in the field of hedge funds or any other domain. For one thing, the corps of researchers in academe and other respectable institutions need something useful to do with their time as well.

For another thing, the politicos in office would be shorn of worthy causes to pursue. Our fearless leaders are doubtless champing at the bit to make the world a better place. Surely the pols are eager to justify the largesse of salaries, benefits and accouterments of office bestowed upon them by the taxpayers.

On the other hand, the campaign of misinformation waged inadvertently by the mass media makes up only part of the whole picture. Moreover, the purveyors of the news never claimed to provide an even-handed view of the world in the first place.

For the most part, the professed role of the press is to serve up newsy stories that appeal to the audience. A case in point is the preponderance of reports on mishaps in the air. In a representative year, a few hundred people at most die as a result of accidents involving airplanes.

By contrast, myriads of folks lose their lives in car crashes. In 2008, for instance, around 37,000 people died on the road in the U.S. alone.[3] Meanwhile, millions more were injured in traffic accidents but managed to escape with their lives.

Despite the plenitude of accidents on the road, the news wires seldom talk about crackups involving ground transports. The reason, of course, is that auto accidents are so numerous and pedestrian. While each fatality is a tragedy, life goes on regardless for the society at large.

If the media tried to cover every death on the road, there would be no time left to talk about anything else. By the same token, accidents involving aircraft get a lot of press precisely because they are so rare.

The astute investor would do well to keep this imbalance in mind. The triumphs in the hedge fund game make the headlines precisely because they are such oddities.

Fixing up Hedge Funds

It would be impractical for reporters and editors to present a thorough or balanced view of any field, whether the subject involves hedge funds or something else. Even so, the members of the media would do well to make more of an effort to present a cogent picture of the world we live in. After, presenting the reality and peddling an illusion is the difference between reporting the news and churning out propaganda.

A simple way to dig deeper into this issue is to turn to a short story. In the yarn to follow, a wiseacre conducts a flaky survey couched as an impartial study.

A Tale of Two Worlds

In the opening scene, the hero of the story places a display ad in a local newspaper. The notice invites readers who play the sweepstakes to come forth and talk about their experiences.

In response to the ad, a bunch of people call in and ask what the announcement is all about. Moreover, the callers want to know what's in it for them.

The author of the message explains that he's performing background research in order to write an article on the subject. The only thing that he has to offer in return is a chance for the caller to tell their story.

Given the dearth of incentive, most of the inquirers decide to back away. "Thanks but no thanks", they reply.

Despite the lack of enthusiasm, the project does bear a bit of fruit. A couple of callers agree to come in and share their experiences.

The next scene takes places in a private room reserved at the local library. The first respondent shows up for the interview right on schedule.

The visitor closes the door behind him and casts a furtive glance round the room. At length he takes a seat across the table from the pollster.

The newcomer takes out a small bottle from his knapsack, and takes a sip of water. Then he looks up at the interviewer.
    "My name's Duff", he murmurs. "Last year, I earned five thousand bucks from the lottery."
    "Congratulations", says the prober. "Have you ever won anything else in the the lottery?"
    "Nope, never. That was the first and only time it paid off."

14

"How long have you been playing the lottery?"

"I don't like to talk about that."

"Why not?"

"My friends think I'm a dope for fooling around with the raffles."

"Well, I don't share their views. So you can speak freely with me."

"Okay, you seem like a nice guy. I've been playing the numbers for the past ten years."

"How much have you spent on the sweepstakes?"

"I'd say about a hundred bucks per year."

"Let me see if I got this right. You paid out a total of a thousand dollars over the past decade, and you got back exactly five grand in payouts. So the net intake during your betting career was four grand. Is that right?"

"You got it."

"Let's see how it works out at an annual rate. Over the past decade, your profit came out to four hundred bucks a year on average. On the other hand, you had to shell out a hundred bucks each year. Based on these figures, we could say that your average return on investment was 400 percent a year."

"I suppose you're right – Hey, by the way, you're not going to tell my wife about this, are ya?"

"She doesn't know anything about your betting habit?"

"Nah, not really. The only time I mentioned it was right after I hit paydirt last year. I thought she'd be jumping for joy cause of all the money I made. But no, she gets all huffy and upset instead. I just don't understand that woman, she's got no vision at all. Ya know, I explained to her, I was only trying to invest in our future. But she blows her top and shrieks at me, Don't you ever play the numbers game again!"

"She sounds pretty opinionated."

"You can say that again. Now ya know why I don't talk to her about my investment program with the lottery."

"You can rest assured that your wife will never hear about your dealings from me. My lips are sealed."

At this point, the second visitor arrives on the scene. She introduces herself as Doll and plops herself down on a chair next to Duff.

"I made $600 bucks last year", she blurts out.

"That's great!" says the polltaker. "How did you manage that?"

"I bought myself a lottery ticket for New Year's Day. It was just a lark, I never thought I'd hit the jackpot."

"How much did you pay for the ticket?"

"A single dollar."

"How long have you been doing this?"

"I haven't. That was my very first time."

"And it was your lucky day indeed. Your return on investment was nearly 60,000 percent!"

"Tell me about it."

"What will you do now with the money you've earned?"

"It's obvious what I should do. I'm going to get serious and invest the money, all of it. I'll spend the whole lot on lottery tickets come the New Year."

"And what about the year after that? How long do you plan to keep reinvesting your profits?"

"For the rest of my life, or until I'm filthy rich, whichever comes first."

"If you keep rolling in the dough like that, I can tell you, it won't be long before you've got more money than you know what to do with."

"You're right, you've got a point. So maybe I'll stop that racket after a while. After all, I'll be worth billions and billions just a few years down the road!"

At this juncture, Duff turns his head and leans toward her. "Did you know that you can buy lottery tickets in other countries too?"

"Really? I've never been abroad. Can anybody crash the party, even if you're a foreigner?"

"No problem. I read all about it on the Internet."

"That's neat. So, I could branch out to a couple of different countries. Heck, why stop there? You know what, I could play the whole wide world. What a blast that'll be!"

"Yeah. And the great thing is, even if you lose some money in one country, you can still come out on top by winning the pot in other places."

"Wow, that's fabulous. I'm surprised, though, that other people haven't thought of it."

"Oh, but they have. There's even a fancy word for it – the whole idea is called 'di-ver-si-fi-ca-tion'. But all it means is not putting your eggs in one basket."

"Wow, you're a genius, Duff!"

"Nah, I got to learn about it when I heard about sumthin' called 'fund of funds'. That's when somebody called a hedge fund invests in other hedge funds. And that's exactly what you can do with the raffles."

"So let's see how that works. In my case, buying a ticket to a national sweepstake is just like owning a hedge fund?"

"Right on. Plus, you can diversify across different countries."

"In which case, I'm a fund of funds."

At this point, Duff beams a radiant smile. "You're a quick study, Doll."

"Thanks for saying so." A blush rises to her cheeks. "Hey, listen. I'm meeting some friends in half an hour, the bar's only a couple of blocks away. Could you come and join us?

"I wouldn't want to butt in. You think it'd be okay with your friends?"

"Sure I'm sure, Duff. I know you're kinda old – you must be way over thirty – but my pals are broad-minded. Also, you're a gold mine of cool dope. I want *all* my buddies to learn about investment techniques."

"I'd be happy to do what I can."

At this stage, the two visitors stand up as one. After taking leave of their host, the strategists step out the door and saunter into the fading light.

The pollster now turns back to the table and mulls over his notes. But he has no need for written aids in order to recall the key points from the gathering.

Over the course of a decade, Duff managed to earn an average of 400% per year. Meanwhile, Doll reported a bonanza of 59,900% during the single year she's been active in the field. The average of these two figures turns out to be 30,150%.

Aquiver with excitement, the pollster types up a press release on his laptop. Then he fires off the write-up to a gaggle of broadcasters.

The dispatch is emblazoned with a catchy headline: "Average Bettor Earns 30,150% per Year". The conclusion from the investigation is simply astounding! Everyone should play the sweepstakes.

Thanks to the magic of the lottery, anybody can live happily ever after. With this cheery conclusion, the curtains close on the stage.

At this juncture, the rapt audience shuffles out of the theater. Too bad, though, the patrons must now face the cold, hard facts of life in the real world.

The Part is Not the Whole

People often mix up the whole with the part. On the other hand, the properties of an ensemble can be far different from any of its components.

To begin with, the entirety is more than *any* of the elements. In fact, the whole is often more than the *sum* of the parts.

From a different stance, a bunch of special cases is unlikely to represent an entire category. The difference between the sample and the population is especially pronounced if the components happen to be screened beforehand in ways that serve to accentuate a particular trait.

The distorted scheme is like taking the tails of a couple of elephants and claiming that the animal is proven to be a willowy creature. In a comparable way, observing a flock of penguins does not justify the claim that in general birds can't fly.

In the foregoing skit, a bout of screwy sampling in tandem with faulty logic led to a phony claim. In the case of this particular vignette, anyone with a whit of brainpower can see through the bunkum – along with the absurdity of the so-called conclusion.

Yet the same type of bunkum is perpetrated on a daily basis throughout the vale of hedge funds. The main difference is that the audience is kept in the dark about the ways in which the putative results are cobbled together.

In the lampoon sketched above, the average performance of the punters was fully legitimate and accurate in one sense: the mean value of the gains reported by the pollees did in fact come out to 30,150%.

Even so, the sample was not at all representative of the entire population of bettors. What happened to the myriads of punters who lost their entire stake and ended up with nothing at all?

Given the pitfalls in store, an honest reporter has a responsibility to explain the real import of any finding or event. For instance, a database that covers only a small and biased sample does not have the mojo to generate sweeping conclusions for the population as a whole.

On one hand, a zany headline such as the one cooked up by the pollster in the skit is a common occurrence in the mass media. In this context, a sensational title might even be excusable as a gimmick for catching the viewer's eye.

On the other hand, any miscue or hogwash in the headline ought to be redressed in the body of the report. In other words, the bulk of the bulletin should present the reality and explain that things are not what they seem at first gasp.

Unfortunately, the standard operating procedure is to overlook the pesky details when dealing with murky subjects. Where hedge funds are concerned, for instance, it's as if we still live in the Dark Ages rather than the informatic culture.

It's high time to redress the shortcomings. With a bit of gumption, the members of the media have the wherewithal and responsibility to reveal the facts buried beneath the veneer of specious claims.

The truth may be embarrassing for the promoters of hedge funds, but the investing public deserves no less. The purveyors of the news could and should do more than feed the audience a bunch of spiels masquerading as the truth.

After all, the viewers rely on the media in order to find out what goes on in the world around them and to use the skinny as a basis for making informed decisions. If it's entertainment they want, the gallery can turn instead to the cinema, theater or any number of fictive outlets.

Buildup to Breakdown

To an increasing extent, the mountain of leverage taken up by hedge funds jacks up the odds of catastrophic failure throughout the financial forum and the real economy. In addition, the pileup serves to amplify the mayhem when the bets go wrong and the pools go splat.

The end result is to unleash a cyclone of destruction amongst the bettors at center stage as well as the bystanders in the wings. The victims in the latter category span the gamut from investors and creditors in the financial forum to producers and consumers in the larger economy.

In the debacle of 2008, for instance, the madcap bets of fly-by-night operators were compounded by similar moves by some of the biggest names in banking, insurance and the like. The inevitable outturn in due course was the smashup of the entire system of banking and finance. Thanks to the breakdown of the financial sector, the real economy followed suit and tumbled into the worst recession since the Second World War.

Despite the enormity of the threat, most people have only a vague inkling of the perils in store. In the dreamy sphere of hedge funds, things are rarely what they seem. In a realm teeming with sham data, even the touted statistics can paint a false picture of the boggy landscape.

Given this backdrop, the first step toward a solid grasp of the domain is to understand the reasons for the prevalence of deceptive figures. To this end, the next chapter delves into the shifty nature of dry facts as well as sloppy data in the world of hedge funds.

Chapter 3

Misleading Facts

We think of numbers as the epitome of cold, hard facts. As a rule, nothing can beat a bunch of data as the bedrock for a solid model of the world around us.

On the other hand, every rule is wont to have its exceptions. For example, a clump of statistics churned out in a sloppy way can paint a warped picture of any domain. The distortion crops up, for instance, when the tally is based on an abnormal set of readings.

As it happens, dodgy numbers play a prominent role in the vale of hedge funds. The false image of the terrain springs from the following sources of error.

1. **Self-selection bias**. As a group, hedge funds are not required to reveal their trading results nor their asset holdings to government watchdogs or the general public. For this reason, only the most skilled and self-assured operators have any reason to disclose their activities. The rest of the troupe will simply refrain from publicizing their performance, and opt instead to skulk in the dark far from public view.

2. **Survivorship bias**. A hefty fraction of hedge funds goes belly up every year. The good news is that the rate of mortality is merely dreadful amongst the top tier of performers. The bad news is that the death rate has to be grotesque within the ranks of the runners-up and the rest of the herd. Under *benign* conditions in the marketplace,

some 12 percent or more of the pacesetters go out of business in a representative year. Despite the heavy casualties, all the losers are excluded from the usual surveys of the field: the pretext is that the defunct outfits are no longer part of the field of contenders. Since the blowups are ignored in compiling the statistics, the average performance of the survivors is not pulled down by the ghastly fate of the rubouts. This type of hocus-pocus plays into the hands of the operators who drive their portfolios into the ground. On the other hand, the investors who go along for the ride end up with gaping holes in their portfolios; their frightful returns look nothing like the cheery gains pictured by the sham statistics. Thanks to the snow job, even the professional observers in the financial forum tend to believe the touted numbers and presume that everything is hunky-dory in the land of hedge funds.

3. **Backfill bias**. Whether a pool is managed actively or left untended, the value of the portfolio in a free market will wax and wane over time. On the other hand, no custodian would initiate a program of disclosure right after experiencing a losing streak. Rather, the gamester will wait for an opportune moment before trotting out a glinty record of decent results. For instance, a debutante that steps into the public limelight at the end of the summer will brandish its fortuitous earnings from the first half of the year. The same is true for the run of profits over the past few years. Due to this custom, the statistics at the end of the year will incorporate the exceptional turnout of the newcomer along with the lackluster performance of the incumbents in the database. Moreover, the average returns of the sample over the past few years will enjoy a similar boost due to the cagey disclosure of peppy data by the new kid on the block.

4. **Culling bias**. As with business in general, a standard practice in asset management is to set up a fresh-faced

venture when the previous one bites the dust. In the realm of hedge funds, though, the practice is taken to an extreme. A common ploy is to spawn a litter of portfolios all at once then monitor the results over time. The operators are fully aware that some of the pools will turn in better results than the others. At the end of the year, the caretakers close down the worst performers and transfer the remnants of the assets to the leading contenders. The deadbeats are killed off without fanfare, away from the prying eyes of the investing public. The culling process is repeated the following year amongst the pools that happen to survive the next round. In due course, lo and behold: the slick operator is the proud owner of a small brood of superior funds. Each of the surviving pools can boast a history of presentable earnings. Another feature of the survivor is a consistent record of attracting fresh funds year after year. What an amazing performance of steady profits as well as drawing power!

The first three factors above are applicable to the entire population of hedge funds. It's unreasonable to expect any self-serving player to go out of their way to reveal the lousy performance of a blighted fund. In a similar way, we would not expect a crafty operator to continue flaunting the cruddy results in the face of repeated flops in the marketplace.

By contrast, the fourth item in the preceding list could be intentional or not from the get-go. As an example, a shameless rustler has every reason to set up multiple pools in parallel for the express purpose of gutting and dumping the laggards in favor of the pacers at each round in order to cook up a track record of sorts.

Meanwhile, an additional throng of gamesters must surely resort to the foregoing ruse on the fly. For instance, an operator might traipse into the financial arena by starting out with one or two portfolios. After a year or so, either or both of the pools will be scuttled if the results happen to be ratty.

In that case, any washout can be replaced by a newly minted fund. Then the clock is reset and the task of fabricating a track record begins anew.

The procedure described above is a sly and perverted application of an otherwise commendable motto: If at first you don't succeed, then try, try again. As it turns out, though, the maxim may be fine and dandy in the world of business but not the realm of finance. The reason for the disparity springs from the ease of taking a stab and trying out your luck in the financial ring.

Creating and tracking a bunch of portfolios in parallel requires no effort to speak of. For this reason, a hustler on the prowl can easily turn into a serial breeder of brand-new funds. After dumping the duds, the rustler trots out the surviving pools as showpieces in order to solicit funds from wild-eyed investors.

Easy Way to Create a Winning Portfolio

The culling bias described above can be employed by any gamester whether large or small, old or young. The process works like a charm regardless of the skill available or time spent in running the spoof.

If a bunch of securities are picked at random, then the punter would expect roughly half of them to perform better than the market as a whole. At the end of a suitable stretch of time, the holdings that lag their peers may be sold off and the positions closed out. The money freed up is then used to buy more of the winning entries.

The foregoing formula is a straightforward way to get into the field of hedge funds. Even in the absence of a willful plan to deceive, the culling effect doubtless runs rampant throughout the circus of finance.

To take up a simple example, suppose that a gamester selects three sectors of the economy which they fancy might outpace the other niches. The next step is to pick one stock within each sector.

The selected items are assigned to separate pools; that is, a single stock is allotted to each of three accounts set up at a brokerage house. Then one or more shares of the chosen equity are procured for each portfolio.

After a year has passed, the gamester finds that two out of the three accounts have outpaced the market averages. In that case, the plunger might even believe in their superior skill as a canny picker of stocks.

According to received wisdom, a track record in any field is a testament to the prowess of the principal. Sadly, though, this platitude turns out to be a fallacy in the financial bazaar.

The main reason is that chance alone can easily give rise to superior results. The second factor stems from the ease of launching and maintaining a raft of portfolios in parallel. The third reason is that the washouts can easily be swept under the rug.

Thanks to the trio of properties, anyone can concoct a track record without breaking a sweat. The ruse requires just about nothing by way of time, money or energy.

In this setting, it's entirely possible – nay, nearly certain – for a trader to be a quack even if they as well as everyone else happen to believe otherwise. This woeful conclusion is supported by the crummy performance of hedge funds after their rollout in the public limelight.

The bugbear is spotlighted by the grisly rate of failure amongst the top tier of hedge funds. The wholesale demise of the high flyers is a clear sign that quackdom rules the roost in this neck of the woods.

Easy Way to Concoct a Track Record

The previous section outlined the procedure for creating a track record in the financial forum. While the formula was entirely plausible, it was a bit skimpy in terms of hard numbers such as the odds of success.

How easy is it, really, to fabricate a winning record in the arena? A compelling way to examine this issue is to take up a numerical example.

For our scenario, we consider a player who sets up 5 accounts at a brokerage firm. For each account, the punter picks one or more stocks at random. We will assume that each stock – and thus the corresponding portfolio – has an equal chance of beating the bourse or lagging it, regardless of the outcome for the other equities.

After buying the securities for the respective accounts, the punter packs up and goes off on a long vacation. The holiday might last anywhere from a few weeks to several years. For the duration of the furlough, the gamester ignores the bourse in general as well as each portfolio in particular.

At the end of the lengthy hiatus, the tripper comes back and checks on the status of the holdings. Most likely, the gamer will find that at least one of the accounts has beaten the stock market at large. In fact, the laws of probability will ensure that the chance of ending up with at least one winner amongst the 5 accounts is about 97 percent.[4]

Admittedly, a stroke of bad luck could cause all 5 accounts to trail the benchmarks of the stock market. In that case, the operator would have to abandon the entire batch and start over from scratch.[5]

More precisely, the grifter would delete the old accounts and create a brand-new set. The purpose of killing off the accounts – rather than just selling off the stocks – is to wipe out the damning evidence of failure in the financial record.

The rustler can of course repeat the same procedure over and over in order to obtain a favorable result. At some point, the fraudster will end up with a track record that can be brandished as proof positive of their outstanding skill as a stock picker.

Easy Come, Easy Go

To round up, there's a simple way to establish a track record in the woolly world of finance. More generally, the recipe works just fine in any domain marked by a dearth of barriers to entry, upkeep and cover-up.

Under these conditions, a horde of contenders can jump into the fray and join the race with no effort to speak of. In the event of a wipeout, the record of participation – along with the paper trail of smashups – can be veiled from the general public and even expunged at will.

In this way, the performance of the punters in the hedge fund game is grossly distorted by the active culling of the survivors from a large pool of candidates. On the other hand, the fluky record of the small band of survivors is flaunted as if it were representative of the entire mob of participants.

In reality, even the top tier of hedge funds that deign to publicize their performance happens to eke out *gross* returns which lag those of *mutual funds*. Unfortunately, the latter group of managed pools is known to trail behind the benchmarks of the stock market year after year.

While the grungy showing is bad enough, the story does not end there. To compound the problem, the *net* return to the clients of hedge funds is further cratered by a number of factors.

One reason for the shoddy outcome springs from the fact that hedge funds on average trade much more frequently than mutual funds. As a result, their transaction costs are wont to be a lot higher.

The second source of slippage stems from the custom of charging a fixed fee of roughly 2% each year on the assets under management regardless of performance. In certain cases, the fixed burden can balloon to 5% a year.

By way of comparison, a number of mutual funds may charge a maintenance fee of a couple of percent or even higher. On the other hand, such exorbitant fees have become increasingly rare.

The shrinkage of fixed costs stems from the advent of *index* funds which promise their clients nothing more than the prospect of keeping up with the benchmarks of the market. The newer breed of lean funds tends to hive off only a small fraction of 1% each year of the assets under management.

Thanks to the competition from indexed products, the administrative load for mutual funds has dwindled over the past few decades. By the dawn of the millennium, the average rate was less than a single percent per annum.

The third problem with hedge funds lies in the fact that they take a whopping cut of the spoils at the end of each period in which the portfolio happens to show a profit beyond its previous peak. As we noted earlier, the share of the booty usually ranges from a low of 20% to a high of 50%.

A fourth factor involves the immunity of the stewards from their own cruddy decisions. When a portfolio breaks down, the losses are borne solely by the investors and/or creditors who coughed up the money and sponsored the plungers in the first place.

Due to the lopsided pattern of payouts, the operators have all the incentive they need to lunge out for huge profits even at the risk of crushing losses. As a result, it's no surprise that hedge funds have a way of breaking down in droves like they're going out of style.

While the individual outfits bite the dust en masse, the population as a whole has managed to survive and even thrive over the course of the decades. No doubt the single most important reason for the resilience of the swarm lies in the rosy image of performance that happens to be entirely at odds with the bleak reality.

Chapter 4

Accidental Profits

A trademark of the modern economy is a profusion of information. On the upside, a flood of data has to be better than a drought.

On the downside, though, the deluge of facts and figures can make it difficult to pick out the gems of dope from the sea of dross. Moreover, the financial bazaar is so complex and dynamic that a distillation of the nubs would be difficult to digest in full even if it were possible to cull only the vital bits.

To compound the challenge, the statistics coming out of the marketplace often paint a skewed picture of the reality. As a result, the investing community winds up with a warped or even contrary view of the true state of affairs.

Sham Data

Certain types of distortion are, by their very nature, difficult or impossible to pin down with accuracy. A case in point is the problem of self-selection. Since hedge funds as a group are not required to report their activities, any detective would be hard-pressed to come up with a clear view of the extent of the bias.

On the upside, though, a number of properties are easier to fathom and quantify. A good example is the problem of backfill.

When a hedge fund decides to publicize its performance, it whips out a record of profits attained during the run-up to the debut. According to one study, the average outfit flaunted an instant history of 37 months; that is, just over 3 years.[6]

In certain cases, a fortuitous record of sparkling results over a few years might play only a small role in painting a false picture of performance. An exemplar lies in a domain where the contenders have life spans that last a couple of decades or more.

On the other hand, that's not the case in a field where the players bite the dust like flies in a sandstorm. To bring up a simple example, suppose that the average fund flits around in the public eye for a single year before it dies off. Moreover, we will assume for the moment that the instant history of the mayflies spans 3 years on average.

Under these conditions, the track record would comprise 3 years of hand-picked data in tandem with 1 year of unbiased results at most. In that case, three-quarters or more of the figures in the database at any point in time would be misleading.

In fact, the same study mentioned above showed that the backfill bias was alive and well in the land of hedge funds. Due to the accidental history of some 3 years, over half of the performance – in terms of investment returns – claimed by the outfits in the database took the form of backfilled data.

From a different perspective, the bloat of supposed profits due to backfill bias was on average about 4 percent or more per year. In other words, the mean performance of the pools would have been at least 4 percent lower if the database had not been padded with atypical data.

On one hand, the returns varied somewhat among the different types of hedge funds covered by the database. In this light, an example of a grouping was the flock of outfits that bet on special events in the marketplace. Another sample was the band of punters that relied on a market-neutral approach in the hope of snagging a profit whether the market as a whole were to rise or fall.

Despite the variations in strategy, though, the minor differences in performance had no impact on the final conclusion. In the absence of the conditional histories due to backfill bias, none of the subgroups was able to turn in a profit.

Meanwhile, only one of the subgroups managed to eke out a gain with the help of fluky data. In particular, the event-driven group showed a paltry profit based on the crutch of hand-picked numbers.

Even in the latter case, though, the returns were lower than the risk-free rate available to investors from short-term government debt.[7] In other words, the clients of the hedge funds would have earned higher returns by parking their money in sovereign debt slated to mature in the near future.

By turning to the credit market, the investors would also have sidestepped the vicissitudes of the stock market. As a result, the savvy folks would have enjoyed higher gains with lower risk compared to the best-performing subgroup of hedge funds.

When a hedgie begins to turn in a poor showing, it might continue to publicize its performance for a while longer. Presumably, the winds of fortune could turn around and blow favorably once more.

On the other hand, it would be scandalous for a card-carrying capitalist to go out of their way to disclose a splutter of cruddy results for a long stretch lasting many months or years. Rather, the laggards in the arena will stop reporting their performance to the investing public in short order.

The custom of backing out of the limelight can be illuminating. A careful examination of the practice can reveal the extent of the underperformance among the laggards that eventually give up and quit the game entirely.

Skew of Survivors

When their luck runs out, a number of hedge funds blow up without warning while others fall apart in slow motion. If the deadbeats linger on in the database, the ones that drop out in due course are likely to have a worse record than the sample as a whole. By noting the difference in performance, it's possible to get some idea of the bias due to survivorship.

According to one study, the average return for the survivors came out to a compounded rate of 8.19 percent a year. Meanwhile, the corresponding figure for the washouts before they bowed out was 3.37 percent.[8]

The difference between the two figures amounted to nearly 5%. The latter figure made up the lion's share of the gross return of 8.19%. In other words, the bias of survivorship by itself accounted for the bulk of the apparent performance of hedge funds.

Raging Bull

Hedge funds soared in popularity around the turn of the millennium. As a point of reference, the assets under management were reckoned to be roughly $38 billion in 1990. By the middle of 2007, however, the holdings had ballooned to $2.48 trillion.[9]

Hedge funds invest in a variety of markets ranging from stocks and bonds to futures and options. Even so, a large portion of the investments are straightforward positions in the stock market.

The texture of the holdings is illustrated by a probe conducted by William Fung at the London Business School and David Hsieh at

Duke University in North Carolina. According to the study, the latest figures in the database showed that 43% of hedge funds – accounting for 32% of the assets under management – were invested in long and/or short positions in the equity market.[10]

In a *long* transaction, a security is bought and held by the trader. The scheme is in fact the usual approach taken by all manner of traders, be they speculators or investors.

To set up a *short* position, however, a security is first borrowed from its owner then sold in the marketplace. The usual source of the loan is a brokerage firm; that is, the broker lends the asset to the trader.

Under this scheme, the goal of the punter is to buy back the asset at a lower price in the future. If the gambit works out, then the intake from the sale will exceed the outgo from the purchase; the difference in cash flows gives rise to a profit after the security is returned to the lender.

As we noted earlier, hedge funds in general have not been required to report their activities to a government regulator. Even so, any investment firm that holds at least $100 million in U.S. equity assets is obliged to disclose its holdings to the Securities and Exchange Commission. For this purpose, the outfit has to fill out a document called *Form 13F* on a quarterly basis.

A number of these concerns are holding companies that manage one or more hedge funds. By placing these firms under the microscope, it's possible to get some idea of the performance of the hedgies in the stock market.

A study by John Griffin of the University of Texas at Austin and Jin Xu of Zebra Capital Management examined the equity trades of 306 hedge fund holding companies from 1980 to 2004. Not surprisingly, the trading results based on the 13F filings were not flattering.

For starters, the managers of the hedge funds were unable to schedule the purchase and sale of securities to take advantage of price movements in the stock market. In other words, the punters were unable to time the market.

Moreover, the performance of the hedge funds – before adjusting for fees of any kind – showed no significant difference in comparison to their regulated cousins in the form of mutual funds. That is, the gross returns carved out by the freewheeling wildcats were similar to those of the regulated strain of managed pools.

On the downside, though, the penchant for frequent trading amongst the hedgies would result in a higher level of transaction costs. The friction due to hyperactive trading would of course impose an additional drag on the net earnings compared to those of mutual funds.

The burden due to transaction costs, however, was ignored in calculating the performance of the hedge funds. As a result, the returns reported by the researchers were overly generous estimates of the actual results.

In line with earlier remarks, another millstone for the clients of hedge funds lies in the maintenance charge of 2% or so for administrative fees such as office expenses. By comparison, the corresponding load for mutual funds has been shrinking since the autumn of the 20th century. By the dawn of the millennium, a representative figure for the regulated pools was less than 1% each year of the value of the assets under management.

Yet another burden lies in the performance fee which plays no part in the world of mutual funds. By contrast, the operator of a hedge fund takes a big bite out of the spoils on the sporadic occasions when the portfolio does end up with a profit.

Based on these findings, the authors of the study came to the following conclusion.

Hedge funds exhibit no ability to time sectors or pick better stock styles. Surprisingly, we find no convincing evidence of differential ability between hedge funds . . . . We predict that as data quality improves, more studies will begin to question the wisdom of hedge fund investment.[11]

Thanks to the adroit use of hard data, the investigators came up with a batch of revealing results based on the public record. Glum as they were, the conclusions were in fact based on a charitable approach that ignored a number of factors which would have further cratered the net returns to the customers.

Moreover, as we noted before, the bulk of hedge funds hides behind a veil of secrecy. In this way, the operators maintain a screen designed to thwart outsiders in their efforts to fathom the enclave in an objective and meaningful way.

Twisted Picture

In spite of the incisive results, the study described above does not go far enough in unveiling the substance – or lack of such – behind the facade. Rather, the probe paints an overly mellow picture of the field for a number of reasons beyond the ones that have already been noted in the previous section.

The main shortfalls of the findings stem from the distortions due to culling, backfilling and self-selection. As an example, a hedge fund with a patchy record is most unlikely to grow large enough to fall under the requirement for reporting its activities to a public watchdog.

To make matters worse, even a large organization can split up its operations in order to mask its activities. The ease of avoiding the spotlight compounds the problem of self-selection.

From a pragmatic stance, a hustler can pursue the flakiest schemes – marked by the greatest risk – by way of a bunch of smallish pools. A plain example lies in the use of a couple of portfolios, each worth around $60 million, rather than a single ensemble valued at $120 million.

Thanks to the dodgy move, the operator can sidestep the requirement for filing detailed reports to the government watchdogs. In these and other ways, a mediocre pool whose portfolio is propped up by illusive marketing rather than solid performance can easily keep a low profile and continue to fly under the radar.

Another ruse is to set up an offshore office as the legal base of operations. In fact, this scheme is used by the majority of the heavyweights that make it into the big leagues in the hedge fund game.

By this means, the outfit can avoid the minute scrutiny of the regulators in advanced markets such as the U.S. and Britain. An offshore site serves as the repository for the money rounded up from investors residing in various countries. The remote bureau also wears the hat as the formal base of operations for the trading activities.

In addition, a showy operator can maintain an administrative office onshore in order to present a respectable front to the investing public. In that way, the local site can serve as the unofficial hub for dealing with the financial markets. Another function of the bureau is to act as the main mouthpiece in pursuing a program of public relations.

According to the pretense, the bulk of the operations take place in a scanty office at an offshore site. Given the fragmented setup, the cunning operator enjoys the best of both worlds.

The hedge fund hovers within close reach of its customers while staying at arm's length from the regulators. Moreover, the hustler can claim – with a straight face – that the trading activities are supervised from an onshore office.

The tacit message is that the outfit falls under the jurisdiction of the local authorities. If that's the case, then surely the investor can rest assured that everything must be legit and above-board, wouldn't you say?

In line with earlier remarks, however, an additional layer of ramparts can be set up in order to keep the federal watchdogs at bay. The money rounded up from the clients can be split up into a series of smaller batches and kept in offshore accounts. As a result, the trading activities would be partly or wholly shielded from the watchful eyes of the regulators located onshore.

In practice, though, there's scarcely any need for a hustler to go out of their way to divvy up the pool of capital in this fashion. Rather, a standard practice in the financial ring is the blatant replication of an investment pool.

To be precise, a prototype is cloned into a litter of kindred pools. Then each of the vessels is alloted only a modest amount of capital.

One reason for this practice is the advantage to the operator in getting the show started as soon as possible. For instance, a promoter could roll out the agenda by setting up a pool called *SuperDuper Fund 1*. The next step is to round up a pile of money from the investing public in order to fill up the war chest.

When the stash of cash reaches a preset threshold – whether a million dollars, a billion bucks, or some other figure – the operator steps into the financial ring and the fires up the trading program. Once the vehicle gets going, it closes its doors to new customers – until such time as a fresh infusion of cash is required to make up for the losses suffered by the fund.

After the vessel leaves the dock, any new arrival who wants to hand over their savings is steered toward a follow-up rig called *SuperDuper Fund 2*. The goals and activities of the second vessel are identical or similar to those of its predecessor.

If each pool is kept under a suitable size, then there's no need to report its activities to the federal watchdogs. In that case, the operators are free to disclose the performance of any fund if and only if it happens to enjoy a lucky streak in the marketplace.

Prior to that stage, the custodians can just lie low and keep things mum. The also-rans who never make the grade have no reason to go out of their way to expose themselves to the scrutiny and scorn of the general public.

Lying with Data

An apologist for the hedge fund game could claim that the operators are merely catering to the demand for risky products from restive investors. According to this polemic, the real blame for the shady ways of the hustlers lies with the investing public that clamors for their services.

This sort of argument, self-serving as it is, does contain a streak of truth. Before we talk about the tenable aspects of the claim, though, we will start off with the groundless portions.

To begin with, there's no excuse for deceptive behavior in the hedge fund game or any other domain. In this light, a counterexample lies in the breeder and killer of serial pools who flaunts the fabricated record of the survivors as a confirmation of their trading skill.

Another instance is the professional clerk who takes a simple-minded tally of the records in a scrappy database. The joker then presents the average peformance of the biased sample as if it were representative of the entire population.

The same type of mischief crops up in smaller niches as well. An example is found in deceptive reports on the earnings of hedge funds focused on a specific style of trading or a particular segment of the marketplace.

On the other hand, the investing public also has to share the blame to some extent. As a group, the throng of prospects and clients as well as observers and bystanders has a morbid fascination with the unhinged junkies in the hedge fund game.

Looking in the opposite direction, the bulk of the general public turns up its collective nose at demure vehicles that move at sedate and cautious speeds. The investors with an impatient streak reckon that they could simply buy the stocks of the Dow Jones Industrial Average if they were content to be slow and safe.

Given this mindset, legions of gamesters in a hurry hanker after glitzy rigs that dash about at giddy speeds. To put things bluntly, the plungers want to get a piece of the action in a bid to get rich quick.

The eager beavers soon find their dreams fulfilled – or so they think – in the coy swarm of hedge funds. No doubt one source of allure for the prospects is the stricture by which the veiled pools are supposed to cater only to affluent investors.

In other words, the vessels are off-limits to the hoi polloi. And if something has been cordoned off for the elite, then it must be a prize worth having.

Sadly, the wiseacres fail to realize that there's a good reason for keeping the general public away from the swarm of hedge funds. The objective really is to protect the average investor rather than ration any goodies for the privileged few.

From the standpoint of the moneyed investors, the somber warnings of huge risk in the hedge fund game are viewed for the most part as if they were vague rumors without a solid basis. Verily, verily, say the unbelievers, where are all those pools that are supposed to have gone bust?

To be sure, the financial press may on rare occasions bring up the subject of heavy losses and sudden blowups in the land of hedge funds. But the mass media talks about a lot of things, most of which are blithely ignored by the viewing audience.

The prospective clients poke around the financial bazaar but see scant evidence of the mass wipeout of the hedgies. On the contrary – surprise, surprise – every single outfit that they come across happens to be alive and well, thank you very much.

Why, there's better news still. Each and every operator that they encounter is able to whip out a track record of juicy earnings for months on end, and in some cases even years at a stretch.

Wonder of wonders! Clearly, the winds blow fair and the sun shines bright in this corner of paradise.

To any serious student of the marketplace, though, it's clear that the wild-eyed seekers have not done their homework in earnest. For instance, it's no surprise that the investors happen to come across only the outfits that have managed to survive thus far.

In reality, the record of earnings for the survivors to date says nothing about the true state of affairs in the arena. But the gullible souls are determined to believe that the lucky punters in the ring will continue to prevail in the future.

The prospective clients browse through the track records of the operators and end up with the impression that the performance of the survivors is representative of the larger population of hedge funds. As the newcomers lick their lips in anticipation of succulent gains, little do they know that they are viewing a bunch of hand-picked cases involving an abnormal and transient band of hedgies.

As we saw earlier, the statistics are highly biased in a spatial sense to begin with. Myriads of deadbeats have been weeded out, and only the survivors are visible to the investing public.

For another thing, the data is skewed in a temporal sense as well. The buoyant performance of the current crop is a temporary blip that's doomed to vanish before long.

Unfortunately, the pre-sold prospects do not go out of their way to dig out the real story trapped beneath the surface. Rather, the usual attitude is, "I've made up my mind, so don't confuse me with the facts." It's not the most auspicious way to traipse into a treacherous field.

Nice Guys Finish Last

Amid the hustle and bustle of making a fast buck, another type of player gets the short end of the stick. The unsung victim is the rare steward who has the best interests of the investor at heart.

Since the majority of the prospects hanker after dashing vehicles, the pilots of sound cruises can attract only a small band of customers. Due to the meager scale of operations along with the muted rates of return, a principled steward is able to earn only a modest living.

Admittedly, the payoff for running a hedge fund – whether risky or not – can turn out to be princely compared to the average income for the population as a whole. On the other hand, the earnings for the restrained players are apt to be peanuts compared to the bonanza reaped by the gung-ho gamblers in the hedge fund game.

The shortfall of rewards might be acceptable to a small crew of responsible souls plying their trade in the financial bazaar. Yet it would be naïve to think that the majority of operators would willingly give up the yachts and mansions on offer in order to ensure the welfare of their customers over the long haul.

Given this backdrop, the straightforward way for a steward to boost their earnings is to expand the business. And to bulk up the business, the hustlers need to build up the customer base.

To draw in the patrons by the boatload, the operators need to take on bigger gobs of risk. Due to the pileup of dicey bets, though, the odds of survival are stacked against the vessel. Before long, fate will terminate the loaded pool with extreme prejudice.

In this way, the mass of investors that clamor for snappy profits end up sailing against the winds of fortune. If the trippers happen to enjoy a spurt of breezy gains over the short run, it will be in spite of the odds rather than because of them.

Hedge Funds in Perspective

The usual tallies of performance in the hedge fund game suffer from a raft of flaws. A fine example is the warpage due to survivorship or to self-selection.

The crux of the problem lies in the coarse methods used to compile the statistics for public consumption; namely, a slam-bang mashup of whatever data happen to be close to hand. The end result is a biased and swollen estimate of the profits to be had in the field of hedge funds.

On the upside, though, a series of in-depth studies by independent researchers has cleared away some of the smog by taking the various modes of padding into account. Not surprisingly, the results are anything but upbeat.

According to the impartial probes, hedge funds as a group destroy wealth rather than nurture it. Amazingly, even the *gross* earnings of the gamesters are negative when the reported gains are adjusted for the swelling due to biased sampling.

Meanwhile, the *net* returns to the customers are course even lower. The shortfall can be traced to a gush of losses in the form of maintenance charges, transaction costs, and performance fees.

Based on in-depth studies, hedge funds as a group make their money not from investing but off investors. To make matters worse, the overall trove of capital shrivels up as the punters pursue a heedless campaign of dicey bets and ghastly flops.

To sum up, the transfer of wealth from investors to hedgies is a clunky process that cuts down the overall trove of mint entrusted to the financial markets. The grim conclusion holds ups even when the spoils bagged by the hedge funds are included in the aggregate tally. In other words, the population as a whole is left poorer than it was before.

Chapter 5

More Booty for Worse Performance

In the world of hedge funds, rounding up a big herd of clients is not the only reason for taking on a huge pile of risk. A second motive for going out on a limb springs from the lopsided setup of reward and penalty.

At first blush, the matchup of gain and loss might seem to make some kind of sense. The custodian gets a share of the windfall if the portfolio turns in a profit, and shrugs off any responsibility if the pool takes a hit.

In reality, though, the one-sided pattern of payout for the steward – namely, reward without penalty – leads to an unintended offshoot. The turnout in fact turns out to be noxious and ruinous for the hapless client.

The spree of carnage that ensues has enormous implications not only for the clients of the hedge funds, but for all types of participants in the financial ring as well as the real economy. Remarkably, though, the bugbear of perverse incentives has thus far escaped the notice of the bulk of market commentators as well as the investing public.

Due to the imbalance of payouts, the hedge fund game is tilted grossly in favor of the caretakers. Unfortunately, the problem does not end there.

From the standpoint of the operators, the reward for berserk behavior grows without bound. The more risk they take, the larger is the booty they hive off for themselves at the expense of their patrons.

For the hapless client, the expected loss from a dippy pool can increase even when the average performance of the fund happens to remain the same. Worse yet, the mean return on investment can sink lower but still yield a bigger catch for the operators.

For a tenderfoot in the thorny world of hedge funds, the foregoing statement is likely to be far-fetched as well as counterintuitive. The bonus for a steward is paid out as a percentage of the profits. In that case, how could the custodian end up earning more if the average performance happens to be less?

According to a popular image amongst the general public, the financial forum is a sanctum of logic and aplomb for a demure community of cool-headed decision makers. If truth be told, though, the temple of finance is more like a circus of chaos that bubbles over with flimsy props and zany jokers, scruffy vagrants and madcap antics.

The din and dust is especially severe in the hazy vale of hedge funds. In this corner of the financial ring, the wackiness could fit right in with *Alice's Adventures in Wonderland*.

The preceding claim might sound like a load of hyperbole, but that does not make it any less true. The simplest way to see how the bizarre state of affairs can prevail is to look at a specific example.

Portrait of Folly

For this cameo, we will begin with a fund manager named Alex. The operator rounds up a pot of $40 million from a band of investors, then puts the money to work by buying a clutch of stocks.

After a year of operation, the value of the portfolio increases by $8 million. In relative terms, the gross profit comes out to 20% of the original amount.

In line with a common practice among hedge funds, we will take the performance fee to be 25% of the gross earnings. Under this arrangement, Alex receives a bonus of $2 million at the end of the first year.

For the time being, we assume that there are no other withdrawals from, or inflows to, the hedge fund. As a result, the balance of the windfall – amounting to $6 million – is plowed back into the pool. After this step, the assets under management stand at $46 million.

Over the course of the second year, the portfolio rises by another 10%; that is, the gross profit amounts to $4.6 million bucks. For his vital contribution, Alex receives $1.15 million as a bonus.

Meanwhile the investors claim the remaining stash of $3.45 million at the end of the second year. After adding this scoop to the pot, the assets under management come out to $49.45 million.

To recap the story thus far, the gross profit was 20% during the first year, followed by 10% the next year. During this period, Alex earned a total of $3.15 million in bonuses. Meanwhile the combined haul for the investors was $9.45 million.

Enter the Wildcat

To round out the case study, we now introduce a counterpoint. The newcomer is a cowboy named Bobby who starts out at the same time as Alex with a portfolio of equal size.

As a hard-core capitalist, Bobby's prime objective is to enrich himself. Spurred mainly by the profit motive, the punter goes on a rampage and buys up a bunch of risky stocks. The grifter also dabbles in the futures market in order to control a stake that exceeds the value of the collateral by a factor of 10 or more.

Thanks to the barrage of bersek bets, the portfolio soars in value by 90%, or $36 million, during the first year. Based on a performance fee of 25% of the profits, Bobby's piece of the action comes out to a cool $9 million.

The remaining share of the spoils is claimed by the ecstatic clients, who plow their bonanza of $27 million back into the pool. At this stage, the portfolio is worth $67 million.

During the second year, though, some of the bets go terribly wrong. Despite Bobby's frantic efforts to reverse the flop, the portfolio ends up with a loss of 50% for the year.

In relative terms, the return of negative 50% suffered in the second year is only a fraction of the positive 90% snagged during the first year. In absolute amounts, though, the recent loss of $33.5 million lies within spitting distance of the initial gain of $36 million.

The portfolio was worth $67 million at the beginning of the second year. After losing half its value, the pool has shrunk to $33.5 million by the end of the entire stretch.

And poor Bobby: since the pool lost money, he gets no bonus at all during the second year. Even so, the gambler still receives the flat fee for administrative expenses. In line with the norm among hedge funds, we will consider the maintenance fee to be 2% of the average value of the portfolio over the course of the year.

The portfolio was worth $67 million at the beginning of the second year, and half that amount at the end. To keep things simple, we will assume that the average of the initial and final values was in fact the mean balance over the entire year. In that case, the average figure comes out to $50.25 million.

Since the administrative charge happens to be 2% of the mean balance, Bobby gets to keep a little over $1 million. The intake is used to cover the cost of salaries and benefits as well as office space and other outlays. That's not a bad turnout for somebody who has just turned in an execrable performance.

Let's sum up the results for Bobby. His fund gained 90% in the first year, then lost 50% during the follow-up.

Over the 2-year span, the investors' equity crumbled from $40 million to $33.5 million. The painful loss of 16.25% did not even take into account the maintenance fees, amounting to more than a million bucks per annum, paid out to the custodian.

Over the entire stretch, the patrons of the gambling fund lost $6.5 million. By contrast, Bobby earned a total of $9 million thanks to his bonus during the first year.

How does this payout compare with Alex's lot? The steadfast steward turned in a profit of 20% the first year, followed by 10% the next year.

In absolute figures, the value of the portfolio rose from $40 million at the outset to $49.45 million at the end. As a result, the investors earned $9.45 million, or nearly 24%, over the 2-year span. We are of course ignoring a couple of megabucks paid out to the operator in the form of administrative fees.

During this period, Alex earned a total of $3.15 million in bonuses. In other words, his intake was one third of the amount garnered by the investors.

The foregoing ratio of 1:3 implies that the steward took home one-quarter of the gross profits. This outcome is of course consistent with the policy of rewarding the operator with 25% of the spoils after a profitable run.

Comparing the Heedful and the Reckless

To round up, the final reckoning is as follows. The patrons of Alex's fund enjoyed healthy gains over the 2-year period. By contrast, the clients in Bobby's camp had to suffer through a nauseating ride and ended up losing a pretty penny to boot.

In spite of the atrocious results, Bobby earned $9 million, or nearly thrice the payoff of his restrained counterpart, Alex. The hell-raiser lost a heap of money for the investors, but made out like a bandit for himself.

By contrast, the staunch steward kept his greed in check and took up a guarded strategy. The outturn was to reward the investors with decent returns while helping himself to a reasonable share of the loot.

The foregoing cameo highlights the nutty impact of a one-sided arrangement in the vale of hedge funds. In short, it pays the operator to take on humongous amounts of risk while fleecing the investors in the process.

That is the scandalous outcome of the twisted matchup of reward and punishment in the hedge fund game. For the stewards, making money for the investors is not the quickest nor the surest way to rake in the big bucks.

On the contrary, taking on scads of risk and sticking it to the clients is the slick way to earn the biggest jackpot. By adopting this tack, the rustlers can scoop up the gravy even if the investors end up losing their grub.

The perverse lineup of incentives gives rise to loony actions that – sooner or later – end up trashing the assets under management. Driven to the ragged edge of reason by the lust for lucre, hedge funds in their zeal can't help but rush past the bounds of prudence and hurtle over the cliff like lemmings in a stampede.

In fact, the dashers tumble into the abyss in droves in all types of weather, regardless of good times or bad in the marketplace. The gruesome rate of mortality is a logical outcome of the crooked pattern of payouts.

In general, the field of hedge funds is not a place where investors can go to get rich. Rather, a series of incisive studies has shown that the setup is a dandy scheme in which money is transferred from the savers of capital to the runners of games under the guise of legality.

Good Guys Get the Scraps

Admittedly, there may be some civic souls in the financial ring who do their darned best to put the interests of the clients above their own. On the other hand, the carnival of finance is not known to be a haven for altruistic souls.

When a cast of characters skulks in the shadows, it's easy to take advantage of the newcomers to the hunting grounds. Moreover, the layout of reward and punishment ensures that the setup is a mug's game for the unwary.

As it turns out, a careful appraisal of the data reveals that the practice conforms to the logic. The cruddy returns of hedge funds in toto, along with the gruesome rate of mortality, point up the fact that the scheme is a losing proposition for the investors.

The only real question is how quickly the losses pile up. If the patrons are lucky, the pools they select may trudge on for years on end before they slip up and fall flat. On the other hand, many other clients find the happy days to be short-lived before the funds go bust and the money goes poof.

Do the customers lose their shirts now or later? The answer to the question might be meaningful in an abstract way, but the outcome is largely immaterial from a practical standpoint.

Instant Loss

If the hedge fund game is a losing proposition for the investing public, then an interesting question is how quickly the money is lost. From a conceptual stance, the money goes down the drain when a fund breaks down.

The same is true in a formal sense. The loss is recognized by the accountant after the portfolio has in fact crumpled.

Here is a case, though, where the practice differs greatly from the theory. In a pragmatic sense, the patrons as a group lose a hefty chunk of their capital as soon as they hand over their money to the operators.

In spite of occasional backtracks from time to time, the volume of capital funneled into hedge funds has expanded over the course of the decades. At the level of the individual investor, one way to picture the flow of funds is as follows.

For every investor who takes out some or all of the profits from a money-making fund in a profitable year, at least one punter is apt to put even more money into the pool. In that case, the hedge fund on a roll will attract a net increase in capital while the wind blows in its favor.

From the standpoint of the patrons, the cash that has been committed to a hedge fund is unavailable for other uses. Furthermore, the money sent over is gone forever when it vanishes with the collapse of the pool.

In a practical sense, then, a big chunk of the capital put in by the investors is lost to them as soon as they hand over the moolah. For this reason, it makes no difference in a real sense whether the hedge funds go kaput right away or after a prolonged spell.

To wrap up, the timing of the blowup is in general immaterial for the clients of a hedge fund. In the aggregate, the patrons should kiss their money goodbye – in whole or in part – as soon as they hand over the dough.

Chapter 6

Jinx of the Stars

The legends in the hedge fund game have an awesome reputation for performance. In the popular imagination, the high flyers have a way of churning out gobs of mint with piffling risk.

Sadly, though, the vale of hedge funds is not the land of milk and honey that it's made out to be. Rather, the mass of operators take up flaky bets in the hope of making a fast buck, then end up trashing the capital entrusted to them.

Ironically, the gamers do in a sense attain the holy grail of making a killing: the punters fall flat and die off in droves when their schemes backfire. In the end, the porters manage to pulverize the assets under management and leave the investors in the lurch.

In this parlous environment, even the most celebrated pool in the field ended up going splat just like the rank and file. In that sense as well as others, the cream of the crop is not so different from the rest of the pack.

Granted, the existence of similarities does not mean that there are no differences at all. There is of course a crucial distinction between the front-runner and the runner-up: the winner manages to win. In fact, a pacesetter may be able to turn in a rousing record of profits for years on end.

Yet even the vanguards have a way of falling prey to grasping ambition. The payback for the hubris is vaulting greed that gives rise to wanton risk and ultimate bust.

As noted earlier, the root of the problem lies in the lopsided pattern of payouts faced by the operators. The stewards receive a juicy share of the spoils after a profitable spell but pay no dues in the wake of a losing streak.

In this milieu, a great deal of restraint is needed to rein in the impulse for taking up scads of risk. Sadly, though, self-control is a stranger to the mass of hustlers working in the field.

Given the hazards in store, the key to survival is a healthy dose of discipline. The caretakers have to hold back the urge for quick profits in order to avoid a wipeout for a longer stretch than the rest of the herd.

Mirage of Performance

In the popular imagination, the legends in the realm of hedge funds churn out scads of wealth in good times and bad. According to the folklore, the moguls have an uncanny knack for generating oodles of profit with piddling risk regardless of the climate in the marketplace.

Sadly, though, the reality differs from the illusion in a big way. In this chapter, we examine the cold facts behind the hot image of sizzling gains by the spark plugs.

The gulf between fact and fiction holds for the true source of earnings for the operators as well as the full extent of the losses. The chasm springs from a bunch of factors ranging from faulty classification and selective forgetting to foul play and abrupt breakdown.

The modes of confusion happen to be interlinked rather than independent. That is, one type of mixup is apt to compound and reinforce the impact of the others.

Unhappily for the investing public, a slew of actors on the financial stage have a vested interest in putting a positive spin on the performance of the hedge funds. In fact, an entire ecosystem of service providers has grown up around the wheeling and dealing in the bazaar.

The beneficiaries in the toll position span the gamut from brokerage houses and commercial banks to accounting firms and advisory services. A plain example is the heap of commissions received by a brokerage house when a hedge fund churns over a portfolio valued at millions or even billions of dollars.

Each morsel scraped off by the broker might comprise only a tiny slice of the amount transferred, but the shavings taken together can add up to a nifty sum over time. Even if the intake due to a given transaction happens to be a fraction of one percent of the principal, the combined rake-off can amount to billions of dollars a year.

Another exemplar involves the army of advisors that support the hedge funds with administrative functions and marketing campaigns during the development, rollout and operation of the pools. Yet another sample lies in the corps of soothsayers that peddle their views on market trends for the putative purpose of beefing up investment returns.

In many cases, the fees earned by the service providers depend only on the amount of assets under management or the volume of funds transferred. As a rule, it makes no difference to the sidekicks whether the actions of the principals happen to be profitable or meaningful, or even sensible or defensible. The aides get paid regardless.

All too often, the abettors in the wings don't even care whether the schemes of the bettors happen to be illegal or immoral, as long as it's fattening. If the adjuncts can reap a profit right now, then everything's peachy in the la-la land of hedge funds.

In this lush setting, bad publicity is clearly bad for business. The vested interests have a compelling reason to keep the investors coming back for more rather than scaring them off. As a result, the common recourse is to downplay the hailstorm of fatal flops while touting the sprinkling of transient coups in the land of hedge funds.

Thanks to the multiple sources of obfuscation, the investing public is largely unaware of the real nature of the game. The same is true of the full extent of the risks taken by the hedgies.

To make things worse, the investing public could well be its own worst enemy. For starters, the throng of punters lusts after thrilling tales rather than chilling ones. As a result, the audience laps up giddy tales of uncommon coups while tuning out gory accounts of routine flops.

To add to the muddle, a battered client who loses their shirt in a shattered fund is loath to admit their lapse of judgment in having picked the wrong horse in the first place. By sweeping the crackup under the rug, the ruined patron plays right into the hands of the flippant jockeys.

In this way, the bulk of the smashups are muffled and buried without ceremony. As a result, the investing public is largely unaware that a smashup is the standard outcome in the hedge fund game.

In short, the operators as well as the patrons have a habit of feting the grand slams with great fanfare while sweeping the botched jobs under the carpet. Moreover, the whitewash is abetted by the swarm of vested interests in the financial bazaar.

Meanwhile, the rest of the credit for the snow job goes to the quirkiness of human nature. The foibles at work include the penchant of the investment community – along with the mass media that caters to the general public – for talking up the rare coups and playing down the copious flops.

Flurry of Entry, Washout and Exit

In order to examine any topic in earnest, the serious student has to take up a balanced approach that covers the subject in its entirety. The systematic course has been the usual tack adopted in the other chapters of this book.

On the other hand, it can be instructive to pore over the exceptional cases in the field. To this end, the main function of this chapter is to uncover the crucial traits of the superstars in the hedge fund game.

Of the horde of fresh-faced players that stream into the financial ring each year, the vast majority never come into view of the investing public. Rather, the bulk of the entrants show up in the forum and fall prey in short order to the slings and arrows of misfortune.

In this way, the wipeouts exit the stage pursued by a bear run. The breathless pace of rollout and buildup, follwed by climax and denouement, is largely of their own making. During the brief romp across the scenery, just about no one – whether on the stage or off – takes note of the entrance, passage and departure of the bit players.

While prancing across the stage, the also-rans have a penchant for taking on mounds of risk in the hope of making a splash. Soon enough, though, the dicey schemes go wrong and the punters fall flat. The washouts then slink out of the ring and fade into the night.

Onslaught of the Zombies

In the economy at large, the financial sector is one of the most enthusiastic adopters of information technology. The tools embraced include hardware platforms as well as software techniques.

An example of the former is a broadband connection for speedy access to market prices. Meanwhile an instance of the latter is a technique for teasing out subtle patterns from noisy data.

In the parlance of computer jocks, a set of instructions for carrying out a particular task is known as an *algorithm*. This type of scheme is exemplified by a program that alerts its owner when the Dow Jones Industrial Average falls by 1% or more within the span of a single hour. Another instance is a software agent that sells off the holdings of a given security if and when the price reaches a preset target.

A digital agent may buy or sell an asset based on an internal set of rules, without the need to consult a human principal for authorization at each step. A virtual robot of this breed is known as an *algorithmic trader* or more simply as an *algo*.

On one hand, an algo may be programmed to take on a longish position. A case in point is the sale of a stock after the price has risen by a factor of two over the course of several years.

On the other hand, a robotic trader could instead focus on a short-term horizon. An exemplar is a scalper that identifies a fleeting move in the market, then buys and sells the asset in play for a small profit within a fraction of a second.

A foray into the market which lasts for a few seconds or less is known in some quarters by the clumsy term of *high frequency trading*. Until the winter of the 20th century, human traders accounted for the bulk of the turnover in the stock market, whether the moves involved short-term flipping or long-range investing.

A jumpy trader who buys and sells a security within the span of a single day has long been known as a *scalper*. Since the turn of the millennium, however, the role of the human player has been appropriated to an increasing degree by the software agent.

Due to the frenetic pace of transactions along with the heavy turnover, the virtual robots have assumed the bulk of the transactions in electronic markets. As we noted earlier, a robotic agent may in principle focus on long-term investments or short-term trades.

Despite of the broad range of time frames which happen to be feasible, the field of algorithmic trading has in practice come to focus on fleeting transactions. As a result, the financial community often uses the term *algo* – which in general refers to any type of algorithm – to denote a software scalper bent on rapid-fire trading.

Icons of the Hedge Fund Game

Amid the swarm of hopefuls that come and go in quick succession, the field of hedge funds also features a small band of players with a modicum of staying power. The best of the breed can beat the market for years on end – until they break down, that is.

An example is found in the celebrated trader George Soros, who soared to fame by "breaking" the Bank of England. In 1992, the speculator earned $1 billion dollars in one fell swoop by betting on the devaluation of the sterling against the strenuous efforts of the central bank of Britain to shore up the local currency.

At the dawn of the 21st century, Soros Fund Management – incorporated in Delaware and backed by a smattering of offices in New York and elsewhere – oversaw roughly $35 billion under management scattered across a potpourri of funds. The mainstay of the ensemble was the Quantum brand of hedge funds based in the Netherlands Antilles and the Cayman Islands.

Within the latter group of vessels, the flagship was the Quantum Endowment Fund which held $11 billion in assets. The pool had been created after its predecessor, the Quantum Fund, blew up in tandem with the bust of the Internet bubble in spring 2000.

In 2003, the gross return for the renamed pool – the Endowment Fund – was around 15 percent. By way of comparison, the S&P 500 index rose by 26% over the same period.

Depending on the particular fund within the Soros group, the manager's share of the bounty amounted to 15 to 20 percent of the profits. Thanks to this arrangement, the combined earnings for the advisor came out to $750 billion. That year, Soros captured the laurel as the best-paid manager in the land of hedge funds.

As shown by this example, beating the market is not a requirement for bagging the big bucks. Instead, a key to success in the hedge fund game is to have a large pool of assets under management.

Riding the Groundswell

The burst of the Internet bubble led to a smashup not only of the stock market but the real economy as well. In order to pry the economy out of its doldrums, the central banks of the U.S. and other major countries pumped a torrent of money into the financial system. The purpose of the move was to grease the wheels of finance and commerce, and thereby set the economy in motion once again.

The ocean of liquidity served to slash the cost of capital for the companies on Main Street as well as the players on Wall Street. On the downside, though, the cutdown of interest rates to minuscule levels had a noxious turnout. The flood tide of easy money gave rise to a roaring bubble in real estate.

The bloat in the housing sector was fueled in large part by an orgy of loans from commercial banks. The lenders issued mortgages to borrowers of all stripes regardless of their ability to pay over the long range.

The flaky loans were then rounded up and sold off to rabid players in the financial forum. In line with the norm in the midst of a bubble, the horde of zealous punters liked to present themselves as traders or even investors rather than the speculators they truly were.

It was an exhilarating time to be a plunger in the marketplace. Legions of eager beavers, including a slew of hedge funds, cast aside whatever concerns they had about the risks entailed. The gamesters leaped into the fray and snapped up the assets regardless of the consequences downrange.

Although the thunderclouds could be seen looming on the horizon, the hustlers were bent on making as much hay for as long as possible. The depth and breadth of the rampage set the stage for a blowout of epic scale.

During the run-up to the financial crisis, 2006 was the last year in which the stock market turned in a respectable performance. Over the course of the year, the S&P 500 index rose by some 14%.

In this benign environment, the illustrious Soros managed to rake in a nifty sum of $950 million. Despite the princely intake, though, the operator was unable to claim the top spot for earnings.

Instead, the winner of the sweepstakes was a trader based in Long Island, New York. The victor racked up a booty of $1.7 billion thanks to a combo of maintenance fees and profit sharing.[12]

The latest outcome spotlighted the ephemeral nature of the wildcat game, where a champion can lose the crown to an upstart even under tranquil or benign conditions in the marketplace.

Whether the fall from grace turns out to be sudden or gradual, the takedown is fated to occur sooner or later.

A bolt from the blue is spotlighted by the abrupt smashup of a high flyer in the hedge fund game. Meanwhile, a comedown in slow motion involves a stepwise slide down the slippy slope of dwindling returns.

Cheering the Coups and Ditching the Flops

In the financial forum as in other areas of life, a popular custom is to dwell on the good times and gloss over the rough spots. The culling of memories happens to be a pervasive feature in the land of hedge funds, where the reality is replaced by an illusion on a grand scale.

A showcase of the filtration process lay in the reaction of the financial community to the exploits of Soros Fund Management in the currency market. When the operator managed to earn a billion bucks by betting against the sterling in 1992, the financial press as well as the investing public gasped for breath then whooped with cheers.

In addition, the caper continued to grip the public imagination long after the fact. In the decades to follow, the feat was recounted over and over ad nauseam by the business media and the investing public.

By contrast, the financial community has a short memory when it comes to the bungles in the marketplace. As an example, the same Soros lost $2 billion in the Russian markets when the local currency collapsed in August 1998.[13]

The wipeout on the mainland was twice as big as the windfall in Britain six years earlier. Curiously, though, the newfound blowup made hardly a splash on the news wires or amongst the investing public.

Granted, the crackup was duly reported by the financial press and to some extent even the mass media. On the other hand, scarcely anyone had any inclination to dig up the details or to dwell on the subject.

Rather, most people chose instead to brush the flop aside. The prevailing reaction was to dismiss the smashup. Stuff happens – everybody knows that! So what's the big deal?!

Thanks to this mindset, the crackup was duly sidelined in the years and decades to follow. The incident was conspicuous in its lack of discussion in financial circles. The blooper was like a shameful uncle that neither the kinsmen nor any outsiders wanted to talk about.

In this way, the financial community suffers from a chronic case of self-inflicted amnesia. The coups in the hedge fund game are exalted and commemorated while the goofs are downplayed and dismissed.

In the hurly-burly of everyday life, the mass of investors are determined to forget that what goes up in the financial patch also comes down. Instead, a lot of people go out of their way to pretend that the market is a sunny and buoyant place.

No wonder that the image is out of touch with the reality. From a larger stance, the charade in the vale of hedge funds is nearly as pervasive throughout the realms of finance and investment.

Typical Nature of the Crackerjack

According to popular perception, the army of hedge funds earns higher returns at lower risk than the market at large. In truth, though, a series of impartial studies has shown that the punters in the aggregate deliver a great deal less at far more risk than the market averages.

But surely, surely, there must be some exceptions to the general rule of a stormy ride followed by a whopping flop in the world of hedge funds? Sad to say, but any exception is apt to prove the rule rather than refute it.

A case in point is the performance of the most celebrated name in the field: the Quantum Fund. The day of reckoning came on the heels of the Internet craze that cropped up during the late 1990s.

Amid the ballyhoo in the marketplace, the chief investment strategist for the pool placed outsize bets on technology firms. Then tragedy struck as the Nasdaq market, which was heavily laden with tech-based companies, crumpled during the first two weeks of April 2000.[14]

Due to the heavy exposure to the Nasdaq, the value of the portfolio dropped by some $4 billion, amounting to 33% of the assets.[15] Given the scale of the mayhem, Soros opted to shut down the pool rather than face the tough slog of nursing the fund back to health.

It had been a thrilling ride while the party lasted. But the time had now come to throw in the towel and start over from scratch.

The cameo above is not meant to single out the Quantum Fund as a dumbo that ought to be roasted as a mascot of incompetence and recklessness. On the contrary, the purpose is to underscore precisely the opposite point: even the best of the breed resembles the larger population of hedge funds in critical ways.

The latter conclusion does not imply, of course, that Quantum or any other pool displays a universal set of features in every possible way. In fact, no entity in the financial forum or any other domain is likely to exhibit the average profile of the entire population to the last detail.

In the case of the Quantum Fund, the outfit did boast a few uncommon traits. The most prominent feature was the longevity of the pool.

Unlike the majority of hedge funds that traipse into the field then die off with dispatch, Quantum managed to survive for 31 and a half years. We can infer from this feat that the custodians had enough willpower to refrain from taking up mounds of flimsy bets with wild abandon.

For their strength of character, the stewards deserve to be commended. In the end, though, the shaky bets they made were unsound enough to bash in the fund.

On a positive note, the jockeys did avert the standard fate of their brethren: the embarrassment of breaking down and going bust within a few years of their debut in the public spotlight.

Another reason for kudos was a measure of integrity along with a willingness to stick to the rules. For the most part, Soros played fair in the tussle of finance, an arena with a reputation for shifty characters and dodgy schemes.

In the financial forum, more than a few of the shooting stars vault to the top of the ranks by stooping to lawless schemes. In this light, an obvious example lies in cooking the books or trading on inside information.

By contrast, the chieftain at the Quantum Fund turned in a superior showing without resorting to a hard-boiled program of chicanery. While the record was not squeaky clean, neither was it overly scuzzy.

Most of all, the operator managed to rack up healthy gains on average over the course of several decades before the jig was up. As hedge funds go, the performance and the longevity were outstanding.

For a bunch of reasons, then, the clients of the Quantum Fund had good reason to be thankful. On the downside, though, the image of solid profits with trifling risk burnished through the decades belied the ultimate fate of the pool: smackdown followed by wipeout.

Even so, the gamer did turn in a good showing while the fiesta lasted. Moreover, the feat was achieved with hardly a stain on the general image of upright behavior.

In sum, the operator sported a bunch of positive traits as well as negative streaks. In comparison to the rest of the brood in the hedge fund game, the Quantum Fund was an archetype in a number of ways as well as an anomaly in other ways.

Shady Moves by the Poster Child

On the downside, it has to be conceded that even Soros engaged in questionable behavior on occasion. His first dustup with government watchdogs popped up in connection with a civil action by the Securities and Exchange Commission of the United States. In 1979, the regulator charged the trader with the unlawful manipulation of a stock through the sale of shares in advance of a public offering.

According to the Commission, Soros had sold off the stock of a computer maker that was about to issue fresh shares. Evidently, the purpose of the move was to suppress the price of the equity.

In facing the charges, the speculator opted for a plea of innocence. As things went, Soros refused to admit to the manipulation of securities. Even so, the trader ended up signing a consent decree with a pledge to refrain from similar acts going forward.[16]

In the following decade, Soros was embroiled in a criminal case on the opposite side of the Atlantic. In 1988, the trader snapped up shares in Société Générale several days after he received covert information about the plans of a Parisian financier to take over the French bank.[17]

A year later, the regulator of the French bourse opined that no crime had been committed. On the other hand, the prosecutors in the judicial system at large called in Soros for questioning in 1993.

Charges were filed seven years later, leading to a conviction in 2002 for insider trading. The speculator was ordered to pay a fine of 2.2 million euros, valued at some US$2.3 million at the time, for the illegal purchase of 95,000 shares in the bank.[18]

Soros conceded that he had learned about the plans to take over the bank in late 1988. Moreover, he began to accumulate shares in the target firm a few days later.[19]

Despite the admission, though, Soros claimed that the confidential information had played no part in his decision to purchase the equity. With this argument, the trader made a bid to overturn the conviction in France by appealing to a higher court.

Yet the renewed effort came to no avail. The highest court in the nation upheld the verdict on insider trading: the purchase of stock had relied on clandestine information about a corporate raid.[20]

The foregoing incidents revealed that even the composed trader could slip into dubious behavior on occasion. If the path to success in the racecourse is that slippery, how clean and legit are the rest of the chasers in the hedge fund game?

One way to address this question is to observe the actions of government watchdogs in their efforts to uphold the law in a field teeming with devious characters. In the morass of finance, the endless cascade of indictments by the regulators shows that the outbreaks of dodgy schemes and illegal moves are both widespread and baleful.

As in other tracts of the financial world, the field of hedge funds has its fair share of rogues that operate on the fringes of the law. Sadly, the horde of villains seem to have no qualms about crossing the line and sticking it with gusto to the hapless throng of investors.

Small Change into Big Bucks

The buildup to the financial crisis of 2008 was a bacchanal for hedge funds. At the time, a seething bubble in real estate went hand in glove with a feeding frenzy in mortgage-based assets.

To place the events in perspective, we need to go back to the turn of the 21st century. When the Internet bubble burst in 2000, the aftershock kicked off a global recession.

As the economy stumbled and floundered, the central banks of the world leaped into action by pumping a flood of money into the financial system. Given the yearning for expansion at any cost, the general public – ranging from investors and politicians to consumers and producers – cheered on the loose approach to monetary policy. Anything that would shore up the financial markets and the real economy was a lifesaver.

By the middle of the decade, the world reveled in a labored but steady recovery in the marketplace. In the eyes of the masses, anyone that could earn a pile of mint was a budding hero. Better yet, anybody that could rack up a fortune was a veritable saint.

In the land of hedge funds and kindred schemes, the king of the hill in 2006 was James Simons of Renaissance Technologies. From his citadel in Long Island, New York, the kingfish managed to rake in $1.7 billion in earnings.

The gamer's claim to fame was the blistering performance of the Medallion Fund. Thanks to a knack for bagging huge profits, the pool was able to charge some of the highest fees in the realm. In addition to a maintenance charge of 5% a year, the operator took home a performance fee of 44%.

Despite the heavy load, though, Medallion was able to turn in a dandy performance for years on end. As a result, the outfit rose through the ranks and soared to the top of the charts.

Founded in 1982, Renaissance focused on quick-fire trading. An early initiative was the Nova Fund, which dealt only with stocks on the Nasdaq exchange.

By the late 1990s, Nova was one of the biggest traders in the Nasdaq market. Despite the scale of operations, though, the organ was disbanded and its activities merged into another pool called the Medallion Fund.

The latter vehicle, which had been launched in 1988, had a larger ambit. In addition to equities, the newcomer handled other types of instruments such as bonds, futures and currency swaps.

The Medallion Fund turned out to be the company's ride to wealth and fame. Over a span of some two decades starting in 1988, the Fund racked up an average gain of about 36% a year after expenses.[21]

In spite of the sizzling returns, though, the investing public could not take advantage of the performance. Participation in the outfit was restricted solely to the employees of the firm along with a handful of their acquaintances.

Secret Sauce

A big quirk of the Medallion Fund was its role as a market scalper rather than an investment pool. Put another way, the operation was in essence a commercial activity rather than an investment program.

An outfit of this breed has ulterior motives for posing as a hedge fund rather than showing its true colors as a market scalper. The driving forces take the form of attraction as well as repulsion.

To begin with, the term "scalper" does not convey the most appealing connotation. The label conjures up images of scruffy hustlers at ball games who buy up loads of tickets in advance at their original cost, then sell off the hoard at inflated prices to the real spectators who show up just before the matches begin.

Plainly, a better tack for a financial scalper is to don a neutral tag or even an alluring one. To this end, a handy ruse is to bask in the air of mystique swirling round the vale of hedge funds.

In this way, the algo traders mislabel themselves despite the lack of involvement with hedging techniques or investment funds. Even so, the camouflage does not always succeed. In the words of an astute observer:

> Basically, they are the largest market-making firms in the world, but they call themselves hedge funds because it sells better . . . The average horizon on a trade for these guys is something like five seconds. They earn the spread. It's very smart, but their skill is in technology. It's in sucking up tick-by-tick data, processing all those data, and converting them into second-by-second positions in thousands of spreads worldwide. It's just algorithmic market-making.[22]

The foregoing passage conveys a pointed insight. On the bright side, the observation is on the mark about the true nature of the automated schemes used by the short-term traders. To wit, a frenetic program of trading by software robots has nothing to do with the investment schemes that the larger community associates with hedge funds.

On a negative note, though, the commentator succumbs to a common mistake in classification by referring to an algo trader as a market maker. By contrast to popular perception, a scalper bent on high frequency trading can't be viewed as a market maker in any meaningful sense of the term. As we shall see shortly, the hustler is in fact a basher rather than a maker of markets.

Despite the misconception, the foregoing passage does contain a vital point. The behavior of a scalper such as Medallion has no bearing on the custom of betting on assets as practiced by the swarm of hedge funds. Needless to say – but worth saying anyhow – the hustling of a slicer has even less connection to the buildup of a nest egg by a genuine investor.

Given this backdrop, the Medallion Fund was in fact another case of an exception that proves the rule. Under the surface, Medallion was a twitchy broker-dealer rather than a hedge fund in any real sense.

The outfit was at heart a commercial business that took advantage of transient blips in the financial ring. The name of the game was fleecing the market by inserting orders in advance of the investing public.

In this way, the operator would snatch a few dollars at a time, or even a fraction of a penny per share. Any single move might bring in only a piffling sum, but the crumbs in toto could add up to a tidy catch over the course of millions of transactions.

A program of scalping has no real connection to the practice of investing in worthwhile assets. In other words, a hyper trader is nothing like a discerning investor who seeks out undervalued assets or acts on substantive patterns in the marketplace.

In line with earlier remarks, one source of earnings for Medallion lay in its role as a broker. A cornerstone of the automated system was a software agent for matching orders anonymously amongst the buyers and sellers in an electronic market.

Another source of profit was its participation as a dealer in the marketplace. For this purpose, Medallion would examine the books of limit orders lined up in real time on the Nasdaq market and the New York Stock Exchange.

The roster of pending orders to buy or sell stocks at each price level can provide a raft of cues on the way the market is poised to move in the near future.[23] A hustler can then nab the shares ahead of ordinary players and sell the goods right back to the investors a few moments later.

Thanks to these tactics, the operator would slurp up an endless stream of spoils from the transient eddies swirling round the marketplace. The maneuver involved spotting the moves, riding the waves, and flipping the goods within the span of a few seconds.

During each sortie, the spread in price between the purchase and sale of a security was apt to be puny. After myriads of transactions, though, the slim pickings would add up to a fat roll.

In one sense, the mission of the trader was similar to that of a pawn shop, clothing store, or slot machine. The object was to pick up a steady stream of pint-size gains in exchange for taking on the sporadic risk of a weighty reversal. In the latter case, a loss could result from a sideswipe out of the blue or a flub in anticipating the market.

Given this backdrop, a dealer or a broker in the financial bazaar is more akin to a merchant than an investor. In particular, a scalper is not what the investing public has in mind when they talk about the field of hedge funds.

Roots of the Whitewash

As in any other area of human activity, the cheerleaders and apologists for the hedge fund game are fond of trotting out examples of stellar performance. In their zeal, the boosters are eager to pounce on any humdinger even if the specimen happens to be a different type of critter altogether.

A case in point lay in the Medallion Fund and its tight-lipped operator. To a thoughtful observer, the very name of the outfit should have given pause.

The founder was a mathematician who named his brainchild Renaissance X, where X stood for *Technologies*. The tag did not say *Capital*, *Finance*, *Investments* or any of the other common descriptors in the financial arena. The name of the enterprise by itself makes clear that the outfit – including the Medallion Fund – was the handiwork of a technologist rather than an investor.

Moreover, the mission of the firm was reflected in the profile of the work force. The company employed a host of specialists drawn from non-financial fields ranging from mathematics and statistics to physics and astrophysics.

By 2007, the staff at the main office in Long Island comprised more than 200 employees. Of these, about one-third held Ph.D. degrees.[24]

As the name indicated, the firm's forte lay in technology rather than finance. In particular, the competitive edge sprang from digital techniques rather than asset valuation or investment savvy.

Calling a market scalper a hedge fund does not make it so. The same is true in slapping a label in the opposite direction.

Either humbug is akin to claiming that a mayfly can lead a long and fruitful life, then citing as proof the longevity of an airplane.

If wishes were jumbos, then gnats would fly high and live on for decades on end.

It's also instructive to note that James Simons did not go out of his way to claim that he was running a hedge fund. On the contrary, the former mathematician made a concerted effort to keep mum on the subject. A hallmark of the latter was his reluctance to grant interviews to journalists.

Another telling cue lay in the information, or lack of such, on the Web site maintained by Renaissance. In describing itself, the company made no reference to a hedge fund of any sort.[25]

Instead, any contribution to the whitewash by Simon was apt to be passive: the operator just chose not to disabuse any outsiders of their misconceptions. If an outlander wanted to brand Medallion as a hedge fund, then the bluff was fine with him.

In fact, it was advantageous from his standpoint to let the mass media and the financial community bark up the wrong tree. The greater the misdirection, the safer was the secret of his success.

In addition to his own aversion to interviews, the headman insisted that his employees avoid the limelight as well. Moreover, the taskmaster was adamant in preventing former workers from making use of the techniques they had developed during their tenure at Renaissance.

A showcase popped up in 2003, when Simons accused a couple of erstwhile staffers of stealing trade secrets. During the clash, Renaissance sued the quitters as well as the company they had moved to.[26]

As it happened, the new employer – Millennium Partners – had a penchant for sordid behavior. The shady streak was illustrated by an arraignment of the outfit by government watchdogs for a spree of illegal trading.

The fraudster had fabricated over 100 shell companies and created around 1,000 accounts at 39 brokerage houses or clearing platforms while using fake addresses in order to mask its identity and intent. The whirlwind of illegal trading on the shares of mutual funds brought the swindler more than $100 million in dodgy profits. In 2005, the operator agreed to settle the charge by coughing up a penalty of $180 million.[27]

As this example shows, the sinkholes in the land of finance are skunky and weaselly as well as caustic and draining. Even so, we will not dwell here on the profusion of vice in the alleyways of finance.

Rather, our main task is to examine the illusion of performance in the hedge fund game. In reality, the mirage of profits is apt to be hollow and short-lived whether or not the players happen to stick to the ground rules.

Insiders Win, Outsiders Lose

However, we are not yet done with the Medallion Fund. For there is more to tell about the storied operator.

Another crucial factor lay in the organizational structure. The capital employed by the pool belonged mostly to the employees; that is, the principals responsible for running the operation.

By way of background, we recall that the manager of a hedge fund is prone to take on huge amounts of risk. When – rather than if – the bets go wrong, the external investors absorb the damage in full.

In contrast, the Medallion Fund made use of a purse which belonged mostly to the internal staff. For this reason, it would make no sense to engage in risky gambits. By this reasoning alone, we would expect the Fund to enjoy a long and profitable life.

On the other hand, the same cannot be said of managed accounts in which the bulk of the capital belongs to outsiders in the form of investors and creditors. From the standpoint of the operators, the money is simply a means for the handlers themselves to get rich. The hallowed chant of the brotherhood is "Easy come, easy go".

Naturally, the odds stacked against the outsiders show up in the revealing surveys of the hedge fund game. Moreover, the trail of destruction is not simply a wanton fluke or a statistical artifact.

In fact, the ill-starred fate could be seen clearly even in the escapades of a single operator. The standard turnout was portrayed in sharp relief by the disastrous outcome of each attempt by Renaissance to act like an investment fund for real.

Bad Karma

After the turn of the millennium, Renaissance launched a couple of new-fangled funds designed for external investors. The eventual plight of both pools was a stark reminder of the ghastly fate that awaits the punters traipsing into the valley of the hedgies.

One of the newcomers on the scene was named the Renaissance Institutional Equities Fund (RIEF). The pool was launched around the middle of 2005 and marketed as a product for institutional investors.

The vehicle would trade stocks on U.S. exchanges. The proclaimed goal was to outpace the Standard & Poor's index of 500 large stocks by a few percentage points over a three-year period.

In late 2007, the fledgling pool was joined by the Renaissance Institutional Futures Fund (RIFF). The latter vessel would traffic in futures contracts on bonds, currencies, commodities and other instruments. As with its RIEF sibling, the newborn rig would invest in assets rather than resort to scalping like the Medallion Fund.

In 2008, the year of the financial crisis, the Medallion Fund managed to notch up a gain of 80%. Amid the blizzard of trading by jumpy players during and after the bombshell, there was plenty of opportunity for scalpers of all stripes to ply their trade.

The following year, Medallion racked up a profit of 38 percent.[28] Due to its short-term focus, the trader was able to ride the wave on any upswing or downstroke.

In the halcyon days prior to the financial flap, Renaissance found itself in the driver's seat thanks to the convoy of three vehicles. Just before the financial system broke down in 2008, the company boasted a larger pool of assets under management than any of its rivals working in or around the field of hedge funds.

On the other hand, things began to go awry soon enough. The RIEF pool – the larger of the fledgling funds – tumbled by 16% over the course of the year. The outfit did manage to turn in a better showing than the S&P 500 benchmark, which fell by 38% over the same period. Even so, a lot of clients were miffed by the fact that the performance fell far short of the windfall enjoyed by the Medallion Fund.

Over the course of 2009, the return on the RIEF pool was a loss of 6%. The turnout was much worse than the upswell of 23% for the stock market at large.

Back in 2007, the two funds designed for outsiders had combined assets amounting to some $30 billion. As we just saw, however, the pools ran into a wall of stumpers over the next couple of years. Due to the cruddy performance, along with a flurry of withdrawals by the investors, the funds were left with a combined pot of just $6 billion.

By early 2010, the stewards at Renaissance were openly debating whether or not to close down the two funds earmarked for outsiders.[29] Until this point, the older of the two pools had managed to soldier on for four and a half years before the clients deserted in droves. Meanwhile the younger pool had straggled along for only a couple of years before it suffered a similar fate.

Lessons for the Investor

In short, the financial community was abuzz with excitement upon the launch of the newfangled rigs intended for the investing public. Given the awesome reputation of the sponsor, Renaissance Technologies, a mob of wild-eyed investors was mesmerized by glitzy visions of mondo riches. Surely the newborn funds would churn out a cornucopia of profits just like the firm's previous spawn – namely, the Medallion Fund.

Unbeknownst to the investing public, though, the newly birthed critters were beasts of a completely different species. Under the skin, Medallion was in fact a market scalper rather than a hedge fund. In other words, the older entity was in essence a commercial business rather than an investment portfolio.

Moreover, the stakeholders in Medallion were almost exclusively the employees at Renaissance. The pool was closed to outsiders except for a wee clique of perhaps half a dozen acquaintances.[30]

As a scalper, Medallion could rake in money all day long, day in and day out. In fact, a steady stream of profits was all but assured.

Given the dearth of risk, there was no point in sharing the fountain of mint with any strangers. The tight circle of beneficiaries was a poignant reflection of a fundamental principle in the marketplace.

- In the current environment, a robust and prolific venture in the financial forum does not need or want any capital from outsiders.

In fact, the situation happens to be just the opposite. As any financier on the ball will tell you, there is too much money chasing too few opportunities in the realms of business and finance, technology and commerce.

Not surprisingly, the vehicles that were designed to act like hedge funds in earnest did not get very far. Rather, each of the pools broke down within a few years of its launch.

To recap, the money-making rig that was the company's flagship was not a vessel accessible to the investing public. Rather, the so-called hedge fund was in reality a closed venture rather than an open pool.

Moreover, each attempt by Renaissance to act like a hedge fund for real turned into an abject flop before long. In this way, too, the fate of the storied firm was typical of the swarm of hedge funds as a whole.

Fair Weather Hits

In general, hedge funds are programmed to disintegrate regardless of the weather in the marketplace. The punters bite the dust in droves when the wind blows fair, and in even greater numbers when a storm breaks out.

On a positive note, though, the occasional pacer can at times perform well enough in a benign environment. In that case, things go swimmingly until the climate changes, which is bound to happen sooner or later.

A showcase lay in the breakdown of a celebrated outfit in the hedge fund game. The sunny spell in the winter of the 20th century gave rise to an entirely different outcome from the rough patch at the turn of the millennium.

By way of background, we should note that the stock markets of the world advanced at a breezy pace over the course of two decades beginning in January 1980. In the U.S., for instance, the average rate of increase came out to 14% a year.

In this buoyant setting, a host of operators enjoyed a heady ride. As an example, the Quantum Fund rose at a compound rate of 33% per year.

On the other hand, the buoyant stretch came to an abrupt halt with the collapse of the Internet craze in March 2000. Within a month, two of the top principals at Soros Fund Management had to resign after losing more than $5 billion in a snap in the Nasdaq market.

After the flameout, there was scant choice but to shut down the Quantum Fund. The burnt-out rig was then replaced by a newborn vessel named the Quantum Endowment Fund.

Thanks to the resurrection of the vehicle, the renamed pool could start over with a clean slate. The plain advantage of the switchover was to bury the past. From a formal stance, the fledgling fund would sport a track record that was unmarred by the wipeout of spring 2000.

The reborn pool would be managed more conservatively in the future. "If the new Quantum can average 15% a year, I'd be very happy", declared Soros.[31]

The time had come for the operator to pay more attention to sheer survival rather than glitzy performance. The newfound pose would require the hedge fund to tread a safer path instead of dashing willy-nilly into icy tracts. A direct offshoot would be a cutback in gross profits along with a reduction in performance fees compared to the gung-ho approach of the past.

Strangers Might be Welcome or Not

A perennial snag in the financial ring is the misperception among investors regarding the mindset and behavior of a live wire. A fireball that is truly confident in their ability to fetch high returns at low risk does not need or want to deal with any outsiders.

At the most basic level, the building block of the financial forum is the stalwart business that sells a portion of its equity to the investing public in order to raise capital. The money is then used by the firm in order to pursue promising projects.

An example of the latter is the design of a new generation of computer chips, a project which usually requires billions of dollars to fulfill. Another instance is the construction of a factory in a developing country which offers a lower cost of production.

In either of these cases, a huge dollop of capital is required at the outset in order to realize the potential downstream. The firm has to round up the money from external investors because it lacks the purse to invest billions of dollars in a project that requires years of effort before yielding any kind of payoff.

The stumbling block is an example of a chicken-and-egg problem: no money, no product; no product, no moolah. The dilemma is resolved by raising a heap of cash from external backers. In return, the investors get a claim on the profits to be earned by the company in due course.

Where Financing Makes Sense

In the foregoing vignettes relating to the real economy, the cost of the project at the outset is the reason for raising the capital. On the other hand, the situation in the financial forum is entirely different.

At the dawn of the millennium, it's hard to imagine a situation where someone with a modicum of talent is unable to a bankroll a trading scheme out of their own pocket. Granted, the pot required at the start might be large enough for the go-getter to round up a modicum of cash from a bunch of friends and colleagues.

On the other hand, the latter scenario – namely, the reliance on a small circle of acquaintances – would crop up only once in a blue moon. As a rule, a personal kitty should be more than enough to fill the bill.

A venture of this sort lies in a money-making scheme involving a couple of assets of the financial kind. The instruments taken up might range from stocks and bonds to futures and currencies.

On the other hand, there's a big difference between financing a commercial *venture* versus investing in the *company* behind the endeavor. As we noted earlier, a business in the tangible economy might have to raise a pot amounting to billions of dollars in order to construct a modern factory or design a novel line of microchips.

But the situation is entirely different for an investor who turns to the stock market in order to invest in the company itself. Each share of equity in the microchip firm will likely trade on the bourse for a couple of hundred bucks or less. In that case, a punter has to round up just a few hundred dollars before firing up a program of trading on the equity.

Dearth of Opportunity, Not Capital

In this way, a teeny budget is sufficient to get started in the financial forum. At the high end, the punter might have to scrounge up a purse amounting to a couple of thousand dollars. That could happen, for instance, in the case of a scheme that involves the purchase of a futures contract.

If stocks are the instruments of choice, though, then the minimal amount is apt to be a couple of hundred bucks at most. If foreign exchange is the asset to be traded, then a few dollars should fill the bill.

Under these conditions, any go-getter worth their salt will be able to fire up a program of trading while relying solely on personal funds. If a stroke of bad luck were to wipe out the portfolio, then the diehard who believes in their project will start over by scrounging up a fresh batch of funds.

For all intents and purposes, even a destitute person can get in on the act. To this end, the gamester could set up a demo account at a brokerage house for free; or likewise a simulated portfolio at an online portal.

Then the player would trade stocks or other instruments with make-believe money. If the punter take excessive risks just like the mass of hedge funds, then the initial stash of virtual capital will shrink and vanish soon enough.

On the other hand, suppose that the punter happens to be clever as well as cautious. Then the simulated account will flourish over time.

If the returns happen to be bountiful, then the player should have no trouble raising a small kitty from friends and aquaintances. In this way, an adroit pauper could get into the hedge fund game without putting up any money of their own.

If the firebrand happens to be smart and heedful, then the program of trading should turn out to be successful sooner or later. In that case, the portfolio will be able to grow organically. For this reason, there would be no need to rely on any kind of funding from outsiders.

If a trading scheme can generate beefy returns in a consistent way, then the portfolio will burgeon at a dramatic rate. As an example, suppose that the average gain turns out to be 26% per year. In that case, the value of the pool will double within a span of 3 years.

For an alternative scenario, imagine that the average profit comes out to 41% a year. In that case, every dollar will turn into a couple of bucks in just two years.

With this kind of growth, the numbers add up at a dramatic rate. A portfolio which doubles every two years will swell 32-fold over the course of a decade. Moreover, every dollar at the outset will balloon by a factor of 1,024 by the end of the second decade.

What does this mean in absolute terms? Suppose that the prodigy had started out with a kitty of $1 million gathered together from a bunch of friends and relatives.

Then the same pot would be worth more than $1 billion after two decades. In this scenario, the main barrier to further expansion will be the shortage of opportunities for making good use of the capital.

Could the wizard keep up the stunning performance till the seas run dry and stars burn out? Not likely.

A standard practice among fund managers is to close the door to new investors after the portfolio has grown beyond a certain size. Depending on the steward and the vehicle, the threshold might be a few billion dollars or less. The reason for the shutout is that the custodian cannot find enough opportunities to put all the money to good use.

A high flyer also runs into a different kind of headache altogether. The go-getter has to deal with an age-old pickle faced by a pacesetter in just about any field of science or technology, commerce or finance.

The achiever is sure to be besieged day and night by a big flock of actual and hopeful sponsors. The entourage of friends and kinsmen will assault the spark plug with a constant barrage of entreaties in the hope of investing even more money into a successful venture.

In order to keep the mobbers at bay, the trailblazer would explain that the project cannot take on any more capital. In response, though, the immediate retort of the wannabe investor is an entreaty for the spearhead to launch a brand-new venture of similar ilk.

With the passage of time, the predicament would get even worse than that. The whiz would be badgered on a daily basis not only by their friends, but even friends of friends, not to mention the expanding circle of spouses, cousins, uncles and nieces of the friends of colleagues of buddies of acquaintances. Worse yet, an endless parade of total strangers will show up unannounced at the vanguard's door with appeals to accept their money for investment.

Running Away from Investors

Given this backdrop, a true ace in the financial ring has no need to seek any money from outsiders. If the high flyer gives in and agrees to accept a batch of funds from a complete stranger, the move will be an act of sheer altruism or a publicity stunt.

On the other hand, a civic-minded dynamo can get more bang for their buck in other ways. For instance, suppose that the player wants to keep a low profile. In that case, the benefactor can donate part of their earnings to deserving charities in an anonymous way.

By contrast, consider the case where the operator wants to carve out a high profile. For this purpose, the handouts can be doled out amid great fanfare to any number of worthy recipients scattered round the globe.

In either case, there's no need for a truly successful player to meet with outsiders and waste any time in explaining the investment strategy or haggling over the terms of profit sharing. There are far more productive ways for a winner to spend their time, whether in terms of personal gain or societal contribution.

In short, the investing public has an unrealistic view of the motives and practices at work in the world of managed funds. A star who happens to be confident in their ability to perform does not need or want any capital from outsiders.

Rather, the champ will be hard-pressed to accommodate the wishes of their own friends and relatives that want to invest more money. The same is true of the appeals to the pacer from the spouses, cousins and nephews of the colleagues of the chums of acquaintances.

To accept funds from an outsider in lieu of an insider would bring on a litany of complaints from the people who feel slighted. It would be an abnormal soul indeed who could withstand the mounds of flak shelled out by the members of the inner circle.

Given this backdrop, any outsider ought to wonder about an operator who is willing to accept money from a complete stranger. If something sounds too good to be true, the proper course is to assume that it is until proven otherwise.

Outlook for Future Generations

In the decades to come, digital agents will play a growing role in the marketplace. Shielded for the most part from the sway of human folly, the virtual traders will make deft decisions with hard facts and cold logic rather hot fancy or cold sweat.

In this context, smart software based on data mining techniques will continue to edge out the human actor in the marketplace. The roles taken over range from trading over the short term to investing for the long range.

By the second half of the 21st century, the robotic agents will be so complex that building the software will require more than a few years of effort by a small band of programmers. Rather, a large cohort of human coders and digital tools will be required to construct each generation of virtual traders from the ground up.

An example in this vein is an adaptive agent that learns from its own experience as well as external drivers in the marketplace. In this task, the issues to consider range from corporate strategy and investor psychology to economic outlook and monetary policy.

After gauging the relevant factors, the adept robot may decide to purchase a clutch of undervalued shares in a downcast firm. The equity might perhaps find itself bludgeoned due to a debacle in the stock market at large, or a setback for the company in the real economy.

From a larger stance, the purchase of the security will provide a dose of liquidity for the mass of jittery shareowners who want to unload their stakes. By the same taken, the uptake of shares by the software bot will help to support the price of the stock. In this way, the robotic agent will act like a genuine investor whose participation in the arena is a boon for the market in every sense.

In the fullness of time, the virtual robot will surpass the abilities of the human actor in devising and deploying a winning program of investment. In creating a digital agent of such skill, the project could call for a budget of billions of dollars up-front. The situation would be similar to the investment of billions of bucks required at the dawn of the millennium in order to develop a brand-new generation of microprocessors.

In that future environment, it might make sense for the builder of a robotic trader to finance the project by scrounging up a mound of capital at the outset. On the other hand, that time has not yet come.

At the dawn of the 21st century, the technology is nowhere near that level of sophistication. Rather, the type of program that can be built at this juncture is trivial by comparison. For the time being, at least, only a con artist would make empty claims about the need for billions of dollars in order to construct a virtual trader.

And the situation will not change anytime soon. In fact, it's difficult to envision any initiative in robotic trading within the next few decades which would require an infusion of capital from external investors.

Instead, the programs will continue to be small and simple enough that they can be financed in full using only internal funds. If the fireballs who undertake such a project happen to be desperately poor, then they may have to round up a modicum of cash from their friends in order to keep their body and soul together while they work on the project. Even so, the purse from a small circle of acquaintances should fill the bill.

It's important to note that the cameo of the brainy robot is in essence a project in software development rather than a pool for financial investment. The money funneled into the venture will go toward coding software modules rather than buying financial assets. In other words, the venture is an exercise in product development rather than the funding of an investment pool.

Wrap-up of Scalpers versus Bettors

A lot of people mix up algo traders with hedge funds. Part of the reason lies in the secrecy that surrounds each type of outfit.

Another stumper involves the fact that algorithmic traders often refer to themselves as hedge funds.

In spite of the popular image, though, an algo trader is a completely different beast from a hedge fund. To begin with, the nomenclature is utterly inapt.

For one thing, a scalper does not hedge any of its positions. For another thing, the mission of an algo is to skim profits from ordinary investors rather than oversee assets in an investment portfolio.

In spite of the crucial differences, though, the scalpers bent on high frequency trading do share a number of traits with the bettors in the hedge fund game. For starters, both types of players have a penchant for secrecy that serves to mask their activities from investors and reporters as well as regulators and policymakers.

In the case of the hedgies, the investing public has been kept in the dark about the true extent of their shabby performance along with the real source of profits for the custodians. If an investor were fully aware of the massive risks and the ghastly rates of wipeout, they would scarcely hanker after the schemes that in effect represent nothing more than ornate lotteries.

The operators in the hedge fund game are driven by a lopsided pattern of payouts: a cut of the spoils after an upswing but a dodge of responsibility following a downturn. The inevitable outcome, both in theory and in practice, is the uptake of mindless amounts of risk which leads to toxic results sooner or later. Given the bent for unsound bets, hedge funds go bust in droves regardless of the currents in the marketplace.

The mirage of profits in the hedge fund game is fomented in large part by a happy-go-lucky approach to surveying the field. The usual statistics of performance spring from cursory scans of data banks which have been stuffed with cherry-picked cases.

After adjusting for errors due to biased sampling, however, the results are entirely contrary – although not unexpected. In the aggregate, hedge funds achieve the astounding feat of actually losing money whether the weather in the marketplace happens to be fair or foul.

Worse yet, the negative return applies the *gross* payoff from the raunchy program of trading. After accounting for the cost of operations as well as the cutout claimed by the porters for "performance" fees, the *net* return to the investing public is of course even less.

For their part, the band of algo traders differs in a number of ways from their counterparts in the hedge fund game. Even so, both camps share the common trait of earning a living by slurping funds from the wallets of the investing public.

In the case of the scalpers, the modus operandi is to suck up the economic surplus from ordinary investors. In the process, the raiders siphon off billions of dollars every year from each of the major markets of the globe. The turnout is to squelch the total amount of wealth available to the financial community.

The devastation wreaked upon the market by the algo traders is a world apart from the bruising caused by the human scalper that preys on the general public at a sporting event, rock concert, or similar venue. In the physical setting, the hustler is apt to corner only a small batch of tickets. As a result, the outturn is to relieve just a few people of a fistful of dollars.

On the other hand, the operators in the financial ring are not the dilettantes of the real economy who pinch only a few dollars here and there from a smidgen of the human population. Rather, the band of algo traders is a mauler of wealth by the billions of dollars from millions of souls.

Moreover, the band of raiders is a rouser of risk for myriads of investors in each of the major markets of the world. The trademark of the scalpers is to jerk around all manner of financial assets to both the upside and downside.

A move in the upward direction comes from cornering the market and drying up the supply on a fleeting basis. In the opposite heading, a drop in price is sparked by the coordinated selloff of a slew of assets. The impact of these machinations is to crank up the volatility and cut down the efficiency of the markct.

In other words, the algo scalpers pulp the payoff and hoist the risk for ordinary investors in an incessant and pernicious way. By contrast, hedge funds in general perform a comparable shtick in an acute and catastrophic fashion.

On the whole, the difference between the two schemes can be summed up in terms of a chronic affliction versus a sudden accident: doom by a zillion cuts versus death by a single blow.

To sum up, hedge funds differ in a variety of ways from their analogues in the scalping business. Even so, the two types of operators share the common goal of raking in the booty at the expense of the investing public. The upshot is to grind down the efficiency, cut down the wealth, and jack up the risk for all the participants in the marketplace.

Humbug of Anecdotes

For every person that dies in an airplane crash, many thousands are killed in traffic accidents round the world. Yet each mishap in the air is emblazoned across the news wires while the slew of deaths on the road is largely ignored by the mass media.

The reason for the blackout, of course, stems from the sheer number of traffic accidents on the ground. If such crack-ups were reported in full, there would be no time to talk about anything else.

Due to the heap of publicity, though, a lot folks get the impression that flying is a dangerous way to travel while motoring is a harmless tack. In other words, the safer mode of transportation gets the bad press because it gets the press to begin with.

In a similar way, impractical to recount all the rubouts in the world of hedge funds. If the flops were reported in full, there would be no time for anything else on the financial news. That would be the case even if the goings-on amongst the shadowy outfits were fully visible, forthright and clear-cut – which they certainly are not.

Given this backdrop, the heap of news served up by the mass media is heavily tilted in favor the rare but gripping yarns of the winners in the hedge fund game. Sad to say, but the same is true of the thirst of the investing public for titillating tales of astounding profits.

By contrast, the supply of grisly news is severely curtailed. For starters, the principals responsible for the bungling have plenty of reason to cover up the botched plays. Unlike the doctors in a hospital, the rustlers in the marketplace have lots of leeway to bury their mistakes under the cover of darkness.

Atop the dearth of hard facts, the demand for bad news is practically nonexistent. For one thing, a trip-up or a wipeout in the financial forum is simply business as usual. A smashup does not make for exciting copy except in the extreme cases where the blowup nearly or actually knocks down the entire system of finance or banking, or even bowls over the economy at large.

For these reasons, the bulk of the news regarding hedge funds is heavily skewed toward the glinty side. As a result, the investing public cannot help but get a warped view of the performance of the high flyers as well as the rank and file in the field.

Sound Investing as an Antidote to Madcap Trading

The most respected name in the marketplace is a long-term investor rather than a short-term trader: Warren Buffett of Omaha, Nebraska. Since the 1960s, the wizard has turned his investment vehicle, Berkshire Hathaway, into a financial powerhouse.

The doyen's key to success is a dedication to farsighted strategy rather than myopic tactics. Thanks to the sage approach, the shareholders in the firm have enjoyed outsize returns over the course of the decades.

Despite the occasional slipup, Berkshire Hathaway has outrun the stock market as well as all sorts of mutual funds over the long haul. More precisely, the value of the equity in the firm blossomed by 22% a year on average over the prolonged stretch from 1965 to 2009.

By contrast, the market as a whole did not fare anywhere near as well over the same time frame. For instance, the S&P index clambered by merely 9.3% per year on average.[32]

Further information on Berkshire is available in Annex A at the end of this book. The supplement talks about a number of issues ranging from the investment philosophy to the relative performance of the spearhead over supposed rivals.

In sum, Berkshire was able to trounce the overall market as well as the entire swarm of mutual funds. Moreover, we know that hedge funds as a group trail far behind the herd of mutual funds.

As a result, the gap between Buffett and the hedgies would of course be even bigger than the lead over mutual funds. In other words, the demure investor enjoyed a hands-down victory over the jumpy traders in the financial ring.

Mirage of the Hedge Fund Game

The vale of hedge funds is not the land of milk and honey that it's usually made out to be. Rather, the mass of operators take up unsound bets in the hope of hitting the jackpot in a flash.

In this dicey milieu, the plungers traipse into the field to try out their luck, then conk out and slink quietly into the night. As a consolation prize, the washouts leave the arena with whatever booty they could grab during their brief tryout.

In a way, the gamesters do achieve their aim of making a killing: the plungers trip themselves up and die off like lemmings. In the process, the eager beavers chew up the capital entrusted to them and leave the investors in the lurch.

As we have seen, even the most celebrated fund in the domain met its demise like the rest of the brood. On the other hand, there is of course a crucial difference between the achiever and the wannabe.

A champion is given the title because they have been able to rake in a healthy profit for years on end. Even for the live wire, though, the prospect of a wipeout is a perennial hazard.

Given the twisted pattern of incentives for the operators, a great deal of self-control is needed to rein in the impulse to take up gross amounts of risk. For this reason, the key to survival is the willpower to keep the venal urge in check and thereby last longer than the rest of the pack.

But human nature is what it is. Sad to say, but gamesters of all stripes are drawn to rash bets in an effort to score a home run.

The end result is inevitable. Even the legends of the hedge fund game have a way of tripping up and falling flat in spite of the bewitching tales of vast riches swirling round the landscape.

Chapter 7

Ambush of the Algos

The financial community often confuses a creature of the digital era with the older breed of wildcats in the betting game. By common perception, robotic agents bent on quick-fire trading represent an obscure species within the larger genus of hedge funds.

According to the popular fancy, the digital traders act as market makers while adding liquidity and boosting efficiency in the arena. As it happens, though, the reality is entirely different.

As a starting point, labeling a hyperactive agent as a hedge fund is a muff in classification for a number of reasons. For starters, the high-strung trader is engaged in a scalping operation that involves neither a financial hedge nor an investment fund.

A big reason for the misperception stems from a bromide in financial economics. According to the fusty argument, a high volume of trading is beneficial for all the participants in the market due to the increase in liquidity.

As an example, the mass of participation helps to whittle down the gap between the bid and ask prices. Another outgrowth is to streamline any transactions which involve the transfer of large blocks of securities.

Admittedly, the old saw was valid in the olden days when human traders were the dominant actors in the marketplace. On the other hand, the reasoning no longer apples in the modern era when software robots hold sway. On the contrary, the scalping actions of the digital bots serve to waylay the investing public by cornering the market and manipulating the price.

In the digital culture, the impact of overactive agents is to jack up the cost of transactions and suck out the economic surplus available to the entire community. Another impact of the scalping operation is to jerk around the price level and thereby crank up the volatility of the market. The upshot of these two effects is to cut down the efficiency and crank up the risk for the investing public.

Rise of the Robots

To a growing extent, computer programs bent on frenetic trading elbow out human players in electronic markets ranging from common stocks to financial derivatives. According to the traditional view of trading, an increase in turnover swells the liquidity in the marketplace and thereby lowers the cost of interaction for all the players.

This sort of reasoning made sense in days of yore when human traders bought and sold securities using manual procedures. The argument was valid even in an era where computer programs served as adjuncts in the task of analyzing financial data, or conveying manual orders on behalf of human principals.

On the other hand, the benefits of turnover are flipped upside down in the case of software robots involved in a scheme known as high frequency trading. Virtual actors of this stripe do not bother to weigh the value of a stock nor glean any insights from the historical record. Rather, the digital bots simply sniff out the fleeting ripples in the marketplace, then drain the marrow of profits from the investing public by using stealthy spoofs on the fly.

In the first phase of each sting, the snoopers poke around the bazaar in order to figure out where the bulk of investors are moving. In the next stage, the busy bees jump in front of the crowd, scooping up the assets in play before ordinary investors have a chance to execute their orders. For the final stroke, the scalpers turn around and sell the goods they just snapped up to the other gamers.

The practice of front-running the order book in an electronic market gives rise to a number of noxious effects. One turnout is to jack up the cost of transactions for the investing public. Another offshoot is to exacerbate the swings in the marketplace as the price bounces around, making big jumps in quick succession. The impact of these two outcomes is to heighten the volatility of the assets and lower the stability of the market.

As a result, the financial community as a whole suffers from the onslaught of software scalpers bent on high frequency trading. The adverse impact on the investing public is a cutdown of profits coupled with an upsurge of risk.

In short, the trove of economic surplus available to the investing public shrivels up during an assault whose main goal is to transfer profits from the investors to the raiders. Moreover, the campaign of high frequency trading cuts down the welfare of the financial community as a whole by hiking the cost of transactions as well as upping the volatility of the market.

Scalpers under the Guise of Hedge Funds

As we saw in the previous chapter, certain types of outfits are often classified improperly as hedge funds. The prime example lies in the band of hunters known as algo traders.

An outfit of the latter stripe relies on a computer program to prosecute a campaign of bushwhacking in the financial forum. The mission of the virtual agent is to sniff out the movements, dart in front of the action, and scoop up the profits ahead of the investing public.

In this way, the raiders skim off an endless stream of booty as the market bobs up and down throughout the day. The object of the intervention is to siphon off as much of the profit as possible from the investing public.

For the opening act in each sortie, a digital robot fires off a volley of small orders for a particular security. The goal of the maneuver is to ferret out the current leaning of the investing public.

In the initial stage, each order is issued and canceled within the span of a few thousandths of a second. By buying or selling a few shares in short order, the pattern of responses can be used to narrow down the reservation prices at which the honest players are willing to trade.

As an example, suppose that a particular stock has been changing hands at $5.40 per share. Despite the current price in the market, a lot of investors might be willing to pay up to 7 cents more in order to procure the security. In other words, the reservation price for the bulk of genuine players is $5.47.

On the opposite side of the market, a similar situation applies to the supply of shares. For instance, a host of shareowners might be willing to accept 5 cents less than the prevailing price of $5.40.

Turning back to the demand side, the difference between the reservation price and the market price represents an immediate gain for a prospective buyer. A windfall of this sort is known in the dismal science as an *economic surplus*.

In particular, the gratuitous windfall enjoyed by the purchaser is called the *buyer surplus*. For our example, the surfeit comes out to 7 cents.

Looking now at the shares available for sale, the gap of 5 cents to the downside constitutes an immediate gain for a seller. As the producer of the supply of equity, the vender enjoys an intrinsic bonus called the *seller surplus*. For the example at hand, the bonus happens to be 5 cents.

The target of high frequency trading lies in the spread between the market price and the reservation level adopted by the mass of investors. While darting in and out of the market at a frenetic rate, the aim of the raider is to skim a few cents or even less out of each share of stock.

The payoff to the skimmer might seem like a piffling amount at first sight. The intake is in fact trivial when reckoned in terms of a single share.

On the other hand, a slim fraction of a penny per unit can add up to a fat prize in an ambush involving mounds of securities. Moreover, the raiding parties conduct their campaign of attrition throughout the trading day.

Certainly, the slice from each share might be piffling. Yet the shavings can add up to billions of dollars a year over the course of millions of transactions involving trillions of shares.

Nutty Label for Scalpers

To typecast a market scalper as a hedge fund is illogical as well as misleading. The flub of classification takes place on several levels.

To begin with, let's examine the terminology itself. For one thing, a scalper does not *hedge* anything as they go about their business. The closest thing to risk control is darting in and out of the market within the span of a few milliseconds, before the other players have had a chance to figure out what happened.

Secondly, a program of scalping has nothing to do with a *fund* whose role is to nurture a pool of capital by investing in a portfolio of assets. A skimmer is no more of an investor than a forager or a mugger.

In fact, a shopkeeper makes a far better investor by comparison. The merchant holds on to the inventory for a longer period than the span of a few seconds or less that marks a scalper in the financial bazaar.

Admittedly, a modicum of investment in facilities may be required to support the activities of a raider. An example in this vein is a computer with online access, or the rental of some office space.

On the other hand, the need for props is applicable to any type of enterprise. A case in point is a pirate and his cutlass, or a lawyer and her briefcase. For this reason, an investment in the tools of the trade does not count as a distinguishing feature of a scalping operation or any other line of activity.

Most of all, though, the profits of a scalper do not come from an organic rise in the value of any asset. Rather, the pay dirt springs from a proactive stream of frenetic operations.

Thirdly, a scalping outfit is run like a closeted venture rather than a communal pool. The honchos running the operation – at least within the ranks of the outfits that happen to be successful and self-assured – keep to themselves.

The proficient raiders have no need, nor even desire, to take on any outsiders or to take in any capital from strangers. For this reason, a scalper is no more of a fund than is a minstrel or a shaman.

Fourthly, a skimmer can be profitable in a recurrent fashion for an indefinite period. Its mission in life is to relieve investors of their surplus cash rather than pursue the greater challenge of creating fresh wealth.

As a result, the front-runner avoids the risk of investing in worthwhile ventures or promising assets – along with the likelihood of heavy losses when the vehicles break down. In fact, the prospect of steady gains by itself places the band of bandits in an entirely different camp from the throng of bettors in the hedge fund game.

Given this backdrop, referring to a hyper trader as a hedge fund is a patent goof in classification. Under the covers, a skimmer is nothing like a hedgie.

Even so, the existence of distinct traits does not mean that there are no common streaks. In spite of the differences, the raiders in high frequency trading do share a number of features with the gamblers in the hedge fund game.

For one thing, the scalpers often slip into the tricky practice of referring to themselves as hedge funds. Moreover, a lot of outsiders – such as market watchers and financial writers – are wont to make the same gaffe in branding the slicers as hedgers.

For a second thing, both the scalpers and the bettors rely on the unwitting compliance of the investing public. In the case of the hedgies, the hosing rests on the dearth of information about the nature of the wagers by the operators and the extent of the losses by the clients.

In the case of the skimmers, the tactics used in bushwhacking are poorly understood by the investing public. Moreover, the marks who happen to be aware of the offensives are poorly placed to defend themselves.

For a third thing, the front-runners and the hedge funds fill their coffers by feeding on the wealth of the investing public. The basic function of each type of operator is the transfer of existing wealth from the target population rather than the creation of fresh mint through productive schemes.

After all is said and done, the honest investors end up poorer than they were before. Unfortunately, the true nature of the scalpers and hedgers has to date been poorly understood by the general public.

For a fourth thing, both types of predation serve to pump up the turbulence in the marketplace. The reason for the turmoil is the custom of the operators for pouncing on the latest trend, wave or blip. The turnout of piling in and out of the market en masse is to heighten the volatility and thus aggravate the risk for the entire community.

Looking at the bigger picture, the frenzied program of trading by the scalpers as well as bettors sucks up resources in the form of labor and capital. The upshot is to leave the financial community worse off than otherwise.

The same is true of the economy at large. More precisely, the warpage of price signals results in the misallocation of mounds of resources.

The baneful outcome is of course contrary to the mission of the financial forum: to serve as a platform for conveying funds from the savers of coin to the users of capital in order to build up worthy ventures.

From a larger perspective, the fundamental role of the market is to promote the welfare of the society as a whole. The population at large includes the throng of investors and companies involved in the financial forum as well as the producers and consumers going about their business in the real economy.

Sadly, though, the constructive role of the market is not only bunged up but turned upside down by the campaign of attrition pursued by the scalpers. The same is true of the hail of destruction wreaked by the gamblers in the hedge fund game.

Given this backdrop, it makes good sense to devote a chapter on market scalpers within a book that deals mainly with hedge funds. After all, the purpose of the volume is to sort out the reality from the illusion that plagues the vale of hedge funds.

To recap, the object of a scalper is to figure out the direction of a move in the market, then dash in front of the heaving crowd. In the initial phase, a computer program fires off a salvo of sham orders designed to probe the private views of the earnest investors. Then the assets in play are snapped up at bargain prices and sold back to the investing public at the highest levels the buyers are willing to pay.

Raiding for Profits

A concrete example is the best way to highlight the difference between frenetic trading and constructive investing. For this purpose, we turn to a telling incident in the field of semiconductor stocks.

On the evening of July 14, 2009, the chipmaker named Intel announced its financial results for the previous quarter. Along with a respectable set of numbers, the company presented the outlook for the business with a touch of optimism.

In financial circles, the semiconductor industry is regarded as a bellwether for the entire bourse well as the overall economy. Within the field of chipmakers, the big kahuna is none other than Intel Corporation of Santa Clara, California.

Given this backdrop, a dose of good news for the pacesetter is a tonic for the stock market as a whole. More precisely, a cheerful dispatch is apt to perk up the entire troupe of semiconductor firms as well as the market at large.

Thanks to the sunny report from Intel, a host of investors placed orders the next morning to buy shares in a rival company named

Broadcom. One second after the opening bell, the equity for the latter firm began trading at a price of $26.20 per share.

At this point, a posse of high frequency traders leaped into action. Their computer programs churned out thousands of small orders for the express purpose of plumbing how much the investing public was willing to pay for Broadcom shares. Each of the phony orders was issued then cancelled within the span of a few milliseconds.

Based on the probes, the software agents reckoned that a lot of investors were prepared to pay up to $26.40 per share. The robots then rushed back into the market and snatched up hundreds of thousands of shares at lower prices.

The bots then flipped around and offered the same goods for sale to the investing public at an inflated price. Not surprisingly, the price of the stock vaulted promptly to $26.39: just shy of the reservation price of $26.40.

Thanks to the machinations of the scalpers, ordinary investors had to pony up $1.4 million in order to procure 56,000 shares at the start of the trading day. The tab was $7,800 higher than the amount the buyers would have paid if they could have moved as swiftly as the robotic agents.[33]

From a larger stance, what was the impact of the assault on the investing public? On one hand, the damage borne by the investors came out to roughly 0.56% of the amount paid for the shares. On its own, a haircut of this size would scarcely ruin anyone all at once.

On the other hand, lightning strikes of this sort take place all day long in a market that contains thousands of securities. Given the scale of operations, what's the total cost to the investing public? To this topic we now turn.

Haircut due to Scalping

As noted earlier, a slew of bitty shavings can add up to a big stash over time. According to one observer, the operators of high frequency programs raked in some $21 billion in profits over the course of 2008.[34]

Taking a step back, we note that the volume of scalping has been expanding over the past few decades. Around the dawn of the millennium, a handful of high frequency traders were responsible for more than half of all the trades – whether by sham traders or real investors – in the United States.

By 2010, the scalpers accounted for 60% of the equity trades in America. The corresponding figure for Britain was somewhat lower, coming in at nearly 50% of the turnover on the bourse.

Meanwhile, the raiders were making inroads in other parts of the world as well. In 2008, for instance, high frequency trading accounted for 10% of the transactions involving financial derivatives in Singapore. On the other hand, the figure vaulted to 30% within the span of two years.[35]

Unhappily for the investing public, the fraction of trading carved out by the scalpers has been growing relentlessly over the years. Moreover, the mainstay of the financial forum – namely, the ensemble of retail investors and institutional pools – is slated to lose an ever-growing share of its profits over time.

In spite of its bulk, the previous estimate of the loot seized by the scalpers has to be a gross understatement. The reason is that the skimmers tend to be cloistered groups that have no reason to reveal their performance or even acknowledge their very existence.

The best way for a raider to conduct an ambush is to leave their quarry in the dark. For this reason, a pirate would prefer to ply their trade without the surveillance or even the awareness of any of the victims or other outsiders.

Due to the furtive ways of the skulkers, a bottom-up approach to surveying the field is unlikely to yield a credible estimate of the scale of operations. Rather, a top-down procedure in tandem with some reasonable assumptions has to be a better way to pin down the numbers.

To this end, a handy point of departure is the pelting sustained by ordinary investors during the Broadcom caper. By applying the fractional loss in that heist to a larger context, we can obtain a rough estimate of the magnitude of losses for the market as a whole.

On one hand, the squeeze on the buyers of Broadcom stock was an uncommon event rather than a routine occurrence since Intel does not announce its quarterly results on a daily basis. On the other hand, every transaction in the marketplace differs in some way from every other trade.

At this point in the discussion, a chorus of hecklers would doubtless argue that every case is different and that there's no way to generalize any of the results. In actuality, though, the presence of unique aspects does not by itself rule out the existence of generic traits in the financial bazaar or any other domain.

More to the point, the bamboozling of investors in the Broadcom incident was made possible by the only real condition required for scalping. The setup needed for an ambush is a shift in price which can be anticipated to a greater or lesser degree.

The motive force behind a shift in the market could be an internal factor or external event. An example of the former is a plunge in price prompted by the sudden dump of a heap of securities amassed by a scalper. Meanwhile, an instance of the latter is an official release of the pace of economic growth compiled by the government.

The necessary and sufficient condition for scalping – namely, a nascent shift in price – is easy enough to fulfill. The flutter of prices is in fact a constant feature of the financial forum.

At the dawn of the millennium, the volume of trading on the Nasdaq market hovers in the neighborhood of $50 billion per day. In line with the Broadcom escapade, we may assume that the chiseling of investors results in a haircut of about half a percent of the money changing hands.

In that case, the absolute loss to the investing public comes out to a quarter of a billion dollars per trading day. If we add up the numbers, the total figure exceeds $50 billion on an annual basis. And that bonanza takes into account only the Nasdaq market.

Yet there are plenty of other bourses to consider. For this reason, we need to enlarge our perspective.

During the first half of 2010, the combined turnover of common stock due to electronic orders in North and South America came out to some $17.8 trillion. Meanwhile, the corresponding figure for the entire planet was $32.5 trillion.[36]

At these rates of activity, the volume of trading in the Americas would amount to $35.6 trillion or so for the entire year. As before, we will assume that the rake-off due to scalping happens to be 0.5 percent of the principal sloshing back and forth.

In that case, the loss to the investing public would amount to some $178 billion dollars a year in America alone. Meanwhile, the corresponding figure for the world as a whole comes out to $325 billion.

To sum up, half a percent might not seem like a big deal at first blush. Yet the slim figure can add up to a fat wad when the value of the principal is big enough.

The preceding amounts apply only to the equity markets of the world. The estimates do not even take into account other niches ranging from bonds and options to futures and commodities.

The loot raked in by the scalpers of course comes out of the pockets of ordinary investors. The windfall has nothing to do with the efficient allocation of resources, nor the provision of capital to worthy ventures, nor the creation of wealth in the marketplace. Rather, the bounty is simply a covert transfer of cash from the wallets of the investing public into the coffers of the market raiders.

From Gnawing to Gouging

For an asset of any sort, the total amount of economic surplus available depends on the matchup of demand and supply at each price point. To bring up a simple example, consider a stock whose current price is $10.00.

The volume of buyer surplus depends on the price that the prospects are willing to pay, along with the total number of shares desired. As an example, an investor named Cindy might be inclined to pay $10.23 per share. In that case, she enjoys a free ride of 23 cents whenever she buys a share at the prevailing price of ten bucks.

At this stage, a pirate could come along and shoot off a fusillade of flash orders as a means to profile the market. Thanks to the salvo of feelers, the raider figures out that a lot of investors are prepared to pay up to $10.20 for the equity.

For the next act, the skulker buys up the current supply of shares on the market and offers them for sale at the souped-up price. The tab of $10.20 per share is only 3 cents lower than Cindy's reservation price.

When she buys a security at the bloated price, the free lunch comes out to just 3 cents. The reason, of course, is that the bulk of the buyer surplus has been commandeered by the raider.

In the Broadcom heist discussed earlier, the price of the stock jumped from $26.20 to $26.39 per share. The hike of 19 cents amounted to a rise of some 0.73 percent of the initial price.

Meanwhile, the loss to the consumer – and gain for the scalper – was reckoned to be 0.56 percent of the principal. The latter figure is nearly 77% of the relative change in price of 0.73 percent.

In other words, the bite taken by the shark amounted to the lion's share of the rise in price for the asset. In some circles, the cutout might be lauded as an awesome achievement for the scalper: the raider go to filch the bulk of other people's lunch at no risk or cost to speak of. From one perspective, the market watchers on the sidelines could be justified in feeling that way.

Yet, the picture sketched above is only part of the story. We can easily envisage many other scenarios in which the bounty for the pirate is even higher. In particular, we would expect the spoils to grow with an increase in the relative change in price of the target asset.

Big Moves Yield Rich Pickings

To clarify this outcome, we begin with a simple counterexample. The vignette involves a stock whose price rises from $10.00 to $10.02. The increase of 2 cents represents a slender gain of 0.2 percent from the initial price.

The investing public rarely places an order in which the price contains a piffling fraction of a single cent. As an example, most people prefer to send out an instruction to buy or sell a stock at a limit price of $10.01 rather than a pernickety value such as $10.0057 or $10.0138.

In this way, the orders are generally rounded out to the nearest cent. Given this backdrop, the bulk of the orders will have prices marked out in whole cents.

Suppose that the skimmer buys up all the shares available at $10.00. Then they turn around and sell the same goods at a price just below the reservation level of $10.02. In other words, the goods are sold back to the public at $10.01 in order to ensure a quick profit.

The gain of 1 cent represents just half of the overall rise in the price of the equity by 2 cents. Put another way, the pirate is able to extract only half of the buyer surplus in this case.

We have thus far ignored any transaction costs incurred by the raider. An example in this vein is a service fee charged by the brokerage firm for executing the orders to buy or sell the equity. Another sample is an administrative fee imposed by the stock exchange for registering each transaction.

Taking such costs into account would further whittle down the profit to be gained from a minute change in price. As a result, a small shift in the price of an asset can at best yield a slim gain, assuming that the outcome happens to be profitable for the scalper in the first place.

By contrast, a larger move in price is apt to generate a bigger profit for the shark. The windfall turns out to be greater whether the bounty is reckoned in terms of absolute dollars or relative figures.

In this milieu, the fraction of the buyer surplus extracted by the raider is apt to grow with the size of the price change. For a plain example, consider a stock that doubles in value. Depending on the particulars, the scalper may be able to snatch pretty much the entire stash of buyer surplus out of the hands of the investing public.

Thus far, we have been talking about the transfer of wealth from the buyer to the skimmer. During a heist, an unfortunate byproduct is the shrinkage of the total pool of economic surplus available to the entire community.

When a raider jacks up the price of a security, the buyer surfeit shrivels up. One reason for the shrinkage is the reduction in economic surplus for each share of stock.

The second factor lies in the contraction of the net number of shares exchanged in earnest amongst the investing public. Due to the bloated price, the total demand from genuine investors turns out to be lower than before.

As we noted earlier, the economic surfeit enjoyed by investors happens to be less when the shares are obtained in a roundabout way due to the intervention of the scalpers. Another fallout is a reduction in the overall demand due to the hike in price; that is, the higher price tag cuts down of the total number of shares sought by the investing public.

Both of these factors serve to squelch the combined amount of buyer surplus available to the community at large. Put another way, the outturn is a takedown of the overall level of prosperity for the population as a whole.

To round up, one consequence of the scalping operation is to transfer a hefty portion of the buyer surplus from genuine investors to market raiders.

A second effect is to squelch the total amount of buyer surfeit available to the entire community. The cutdown springs from the double whammy of a hoisted price (which slashes the surplus per share) coupled with a shrunken demand for the total number of shares.

In the discussion so far, we have examined the loss of buyer surplus suffered by the investing public. Unfortunately, the buyers are not the only losers in the scalping game.

Whacking the Sellers

Remarkably, the original owners of the securities also suffer at the hands of the scalpers. The loss stems from the fact that the shareholders relinquish the securities at bargain prices due to the lack of timely information on the state of the market. On the whole, the process at work is analogous to the mulct of economic surplus suffered by the buyers.

As in the purchase of stock by the general public, the scalping action cuts down the financial surfeit for the shareowners who sell their stakes.[37] The drubbing takes place as the investors who act in good faith are overwhelmed by the avalanche of orders bursting upon the market.

Amid the bedlam, the investors give up their shares at lower prices than they would in an orderly market where they have the wherewithal to react in a timely fashion to the latest events. The upshot is a squash of the total amount of seller surplus available to all the participants in the arena.

In this way, the combined volume of economic surplus available to the investing public is pulped in an onslaught of the scalpers. The turnout is to leave the general public worse off than they were before.

A similar situation crops up during a raid in a slumping market. The owners of the equity take a beating as the bandits swoop in and snatch up a big chunk the seller surplus for themselves.

114

In order to carry out this maneuver, the scalpers can borrow shares from their brokers and sell the securities on the open market. After the price of the stock has collapsed, a suitable volume of equity is bought back from the investing public and returned to the brokerage firm. When the brokers are repaid and the accounts squared up, the raiders end up with a nifty profit for themselves.

Taking Hits in All Directions

To wrap up, the mission of the raider is to seize as much of the economic surfeit as they can from the investing public. When the market moves to the upside, for instance, the bona fide investors have to surrender a big chunk of their buyer surplus to the robotic bandit.

A second form of loss stems from a takedown of the total amount of buyer surplus available to all the participants in the market. A hefty portion of the windfall is appropriated by the pirates, while another heap is lost entirely to the entire community.

On the whole, the same process is applicable to the seller surplus. More precisely, a mound of economic surplus is transferred from the investors to the skulkers, while another hunk vanishes completely from the marketplace.

The impact of the rake-off is to reduce the overall level of prosperity. In other words, the scalping operation is a profligate scheme that destroys wealth for the entire community during the abrasive process of transferring money from the investors to the raiders.

Quiver of the Market

In the preceding section, the examples dealt mostly with meager changes in price. On the other hand, stocks of all stripes often bounce around by 1 percent or more within the span of a single day.

A graphic sample is found in the chart below. The display shows the relative performance of the S&P 500 index along with a small selection of stocks encompassed by the benchmark.

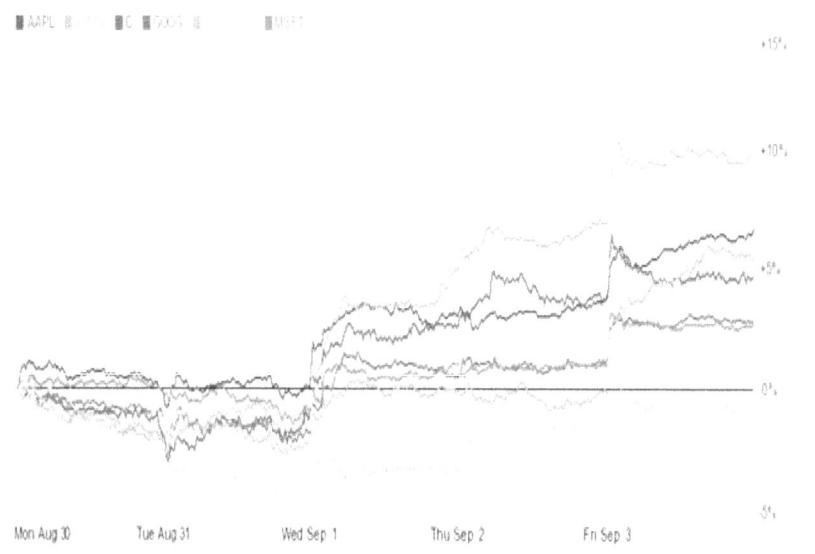

Jitter of the giants. The chart shows the relative performance of five heavyweights along with the S&P index. *Source*: Adapted from Yahoo Finance.

The curves on the diagram portray the behavior of the following stocks: Amazon (denoted by the ticker symbol of AMZN), Apple (AAPL), Citigroup (C), Google (GOOG), Goldman Sachs (GS), Mastercard (MA), and Microsoft (MSFT). These firms represent some of the biggest names in the marketplace.

The chart covers the week ending on 3 September 2010. Throughout this stretch, the bourse as a whole loitered more or less in a placid state.

During the period spanned by the plot, the market benchmark – shown in light blue – started out at a value of 1,062.90. Over the course of the week, the index touched a low of 1,040.88 followed by a high of 1,105.10. The closing level at the end of the stretch was 1,104.51.

By way of comparison, the yardstick had wrapped up the previous week with a close of 1,064.59. Based on the the last two figures, the benchmark rose by some 3.75 percent on a weekly basis.

In this complaisant environment, the volatility was relatively low. Moreover, a composite yardstick – whether it be the S&P index or any other average measure – tends to smooth out the convulsions in price amongst the constituent stocks.

Despite the tranquil conditions, even the benchmark bounced around by a goodly amount. On four of the five days, the S&P index reached a peak which was more than 1 percent higher than the trough for the same day.

Only on one occasion was the churning of the benchmark more subdued. On Thursday, the ceiling was about 0.9 percent higher than the floor for the day.

On the other hand, the temporary calm was broken at once by a hefty shift. After rising slowly on Thursday afternoon, the index shot upward at the beginning of the next day.

As to be expected, the individual stocks within the benchmark were prone to higher levels of turbulence than the average level tracked by the index. The commotion is plainly visible even in the current sample which happens to represent a demure selection: the equities showcased here belong to large and stable firms.

The S&P benchmark covers 500 of the biggest names in the stock market. Yet there are roughly 10,000 companies listed in the U.S. alone.

Most of the firms in the stock market are far smaller than the giants covered by the S&P index. Due to the higher risk of bankruptcy, the small fry tend to be a lot more fidgety than the big fish.

For this reason, the relative swings in price for the minnows are wont to be far greater. Given the magnitude of the moves, the algo traders have a lot more room to ply their trade. In other words, the scalpers would in general find it easier to slice off bigger chunks of economic surplus from the vast majority of stocks listed on the bourse.

Given this backdrop, the rake-off of billions of dollars that we talked about earlier has to be a gross underestimate. In reality the raiders have the motive, the opportunity, and the means to carve out far bigger hunks of the pie for themselves at the expense of the general public.

Private Gain and Communal Loss

In days of yore, a high volume of trading was seen as a hearty sign of a sprightly market. Due to the liquidity in the market, an investor would find it easy to procure a large block of shares without causing the price to swell by a huge amount. By the same token, a seller could unload their holdings in short order without slamming the price.

Based on this argument, an abundance of turnover was viewed as a boon for all the participants. Sadly, though, the happy outcome crops up only when the participants are genuine investors who engage in a welter of independent transactions prompted by a diverse set of views.

By contrast, the wholesome result does not ensue when the blizzard of trading involves a deliberate campaign of fleecing the investing public by jerking around the assets in the marketplace.

As we have seen, each sally by a raider involves a tricky hail of orders and trades whose aim is to corner the market and thereby manipulate the price in short bursts.

For this reason, a program of scalping is a stark exception to the general rule of efficiency through lively trading. In fact, the cost to the investing public rises rather than falls as a result of the double-dealing. Put another way, the impact of high frequency trading is to increase the friction in the market rather than streamline the transactions.

In addition, the scalpers add to the turmoil in the forum by rushing in and out of the market en masse. Another factor is a deliberate and abrupt shift in price – rather than the smooth trend in the absence of hustling – to the worst level that the mass of investors will tolerate.

Under normal circumstances, the market tends to move gradually in the form of gentle waves or orderly trends. When a scalper tampers with the workings of the market, though, the price is unable to move naturally or gradually. Rather, the turnout is a series of sudden breaks which causes the market to lurch up and down in a spasmodic way.

To make matters worse, the purchase or sale of large blocks of assets in a rush is apt to shove the price level beyond any sensible range. As an example, a gang of raiders that jump on the bandwagon during an uptrend is bound to push up the price too far, too fast.

When a bloated trend runs out of steam, the mass of assets scooped up by the manipulators will have to be jettisoned at some point. After the market has stalled, the speculators have no reason to hang on to the goods any longer.

At this stage, the scalpers jostle each other in a frantic effort to unload their holdings before everybody else. The headlong flight out of the market then causes the price to dive.

In a nutshell, the scalping scheme can be pictured as a swift, wild fling in which a bubble is stoked then capped by a blowup followed by a meltdown. As a result, the turmoil in the market is aggravated to no good end. The upshot is to jack up the risk for all the participants in the market.

To round up, a large volume of transactions can be a healthy feature of the market when the actors are forthright investors who buy and sell their wares based on a multiplicity of independent views. On the other hand, the benefits of turnover are flipped upside down when a bunch of raiders add to the tumult by pouncing on the latest move in order to corner the market and shanghai the price.

Instead of streamlining the bourse, the raiders gum it up by nabbing the assets then dumping them en masse. In jerking the price around, the scalpers subvert the proper role of the market as a conduit for the sound allocation of resources.

Moreover, the sudden entry and exit of the plungers whips up the volatility in the marketplace. The impact is to exacerbate the risk of participation for the financial community as a whole.

Market Maker versus Front-Runner

On the floor of the New York Stock Exchange, a human agent known as a *specialist* serves as an auctioneer for the securities listed on the bourse. Each mediator of this stripe is charged with the task of lining up buyers and sellers on the fly for a small set of stocks.

Much of the time, the professional simply names a price for the purpose of matching up the demand against the supply of shares from sundry parties. In the process, the intermediary acts as a *broker* amongst the principals who trade with each other.

Another vital function of the specialist is to temper the gyrations in price by keeping a tight spread between the bid and ask prices for each stock under their care. To this end, the stalwart stands ready to buy shares from all comers at the announced price, and to sell the equity at a slightly higher level.

When the mediator handles an inventory of stock, they act as a *dealer* for the security. While assuming this role, the principal reaps a profit from the small difference between the bid and offer prices.

In this setting, no one refers to the specialist as a hedge fund or an investment pool. At heart, the role of the mediator is to run a business rather than manage a portfolio.

Of course, the professional might decide to hang on to a particular clutch of shares for a personal portfolio over the span of a few days or weeks, or even months or years. On the other hand, a position of this sort is a private move that has nothing to do with their metier as a broker or a dealer.

Rather, a long-range holding happens to be an extrinsic action stemming from the persona of the specialist as an independent investor. In other words, the acquisition has no bearing on their role as a service provider on the floor of the stock exchange.

Poking, Jerking and Leeching

In the olden days, a dealer who bought and sold securities throughout the day enabled other participants to trade a large number of shares with swiftness and efficiency. An actor of this stripe could fulfill their function in person, as in the case of a specialist on the floor of the New York Stock Exchange. Or the agent might pursue their role from afar, as in the likes of a remote trader working the Nasdaq market from a laptop in a remote country.

The steady stream of transactions by a dealer serves to streamline the flow of transactions. Thanks to the liquidity, the investing public can avoid the high cost of trading that prevails within a thin market marked by skimpy volume.

In this milieu, a dealer lifts the productivity of the investing public and boosts the vitality of the stock market. Meanwhile, a broker serves as a mediator in matching up other traders with each other. For these reasons, a broker or a dealer is known as a *market maker*.

By contrast, the automated programs that engage in high frequency trading have the opposite effect. Granted, the software bots do crank up the volume of transactions in the marketplace. At first blush, the increase in turnover might seem like a good thing for the market.

On the other hand, the scalper fixes the price after conducting a stealthy probe of the investing public. After the scan, the skulker rounds up a heap of shares for the express purpose of removing them from the general supply available at the prevailing price.

The next step is to ransom the hijacked shares at the highest level that the mass of investors is willing to bear. The sneaky scheme stands in stark contrast to the free flow of information that makes for a healthy market.

In short, the scalper fires off a volley of sham orders, ferrets out the reservation prices amongst the investing public, and sets the price at the worst level that the market will tolerate. When the bourse is trending upward, the price chosen is a mite below the maximum price that will clear the amassed supply of shares against the demand from genuine investors.

The picture is analogous in the converse case when the market is moving in the downward direction. In particular, a raider can borrow shares from their brokerage firm and dump the securities on the market with the intention of buying back the goods after the price has collapsed.

During each of these moves, the market jerker turns a gradual trend into a sudden jump. As a result, the investing public takes a beating in the process of buying a security as well as selling it.

Moreover, the market is apt to overreach the sensible range of prices when a band of hustlers rushes in or out of the market en masse. Amid the commotion, the thrash of prices turns out to be more severe than it would be in the absence of the raids.

Due to the sudden shifts and the exaggerated moves in price, the campaign of scalping pumps up the turbulence in the marketplace. The process belies the role of a market maker in any sense of the label. On the contrary, the chiseling of the skimmers throws a monkey wrench into the machinery of the marketplace.

Making or Breaking the Market

On the whole, digital technology provides a wealth of benefits for the financial forum as well as the real economy. On the other hand, a program of robotic scalping is one of the rare ways in which a computer system can clog up the flow of transactions and cut down the welfare of the larger community.

A second offshoot is the upsurge of volatility in the marketplace. The impact of the two bogeys – namely, friction and turbulence – is to slash the payoff and hike the risk for the entire community.

In these ways, the digital ploy leads to a net loss for the financial arena. Another millstone is the toll on the real economy which relies on the efficiency and stability of the capital markets for the proper allocation of resources from the savers of coin to the users of funds.

Some folks have the impression that crafty software and brawny hardware are responsible for the pernicious effects of high frequency trading. Amid the havoc and the muddle, though, it's important to lay the blame where it really belongs. Like any other type of instrument, a computer can be used for good or ill.

It seems fair to say that an inanimate tool does not lay waste to the environs of its own volition. Rather, the authority and responsibility for any mayhem belong to the human forger that deploys the contraption in a productive or destructive fashion.

Moral of the Shtick

A program of high frequency trading cuts down the efficiency of transactions in the financial ring. Moreover the price level lurches up and down while taking outsize steps in quick succession. As a result, the investing public ends up paying more while facing a rougher ride than they would in the absence of the software bots.

Some people use the term *market maker* to denote any actor that buys and sells securities throughout the day. In the olden days, such a player did in fact contribute to the smooth flow of transactions and pare down the cost of trading for the investing public.

On the other hand, the software agents engaged in high frequency trading have precisely the opposite effect. The virtual zombies jack up the cost of transactions for the investing public while cranking up the turbulence in the marketplace.

The upshot is lower returns and heighten risk for the financial community as a whole. For these reasons, a robotic drudge of this ilk is not much of a market maker. Rather, a better epithet would be a *market sacker*.

Games of Positive and Negative Sum

Looking at the big picture, the role of the financial forum is to bring together the suppliers and users of capital. For instance, an investor with some spare cash funnels the money into the stock market so that the funds can be put to good use by upright firms in the pursuit of worthy ventures.

For their part, the users of capital obtain the funding needed to pursue promising projects while their backers share in the earnings that ensue in due course. In this way, everyone benefits from an exchange of assets in good faith.

In the short run, the mutual gains for the participants are reflected in the economic surplus generated by each transaction. In particular, a surfeit is enjoyed by the firm that issues stock as well as the investor who buys the equity.

From a longer perspective, the enterprise has the opportunity to build up its business. With the passage of time, the shareowners partake of the income generated by the products. Meanwhile the consumers in the real economy enjoy their own dose of buyer surplus upon the purchase of the widgets.

In these ways, the financial forum creates a net gain for each group of earnest participants. The benefits crop up over a multiplicity of time frames: the near term, mid range, long run, or a combo of horizons. In the parlance of the economist, the transactions add up to a positive sum for every type of actor in the marketplace.

The boons of the bourse crop up in other types of markets as well. A case in point is the futures market.

As an example, a producer of petroleum might sell a futures contract on crude oil in order to protect its revenues from a potential drop in price a few months down the line. On the opposite side of the transaction, a refinery could buy the selfsame contract in order to secure an adequate supply of fodder at a reasonable cost even if the market price of the commodity were to rise downrange. In this way, the buyer as well as the seller of the contract enjoy a dollop of economic surplus.

More generally, each type of market is on the whole a positive sum game. Unfortunately, the same cannot be said of certain gamesters and their monkey business in the bazaar.

As we have seen, the scalpers have a way of squelching the total amount of economic surplus available to the entire community. To compound the mischief, the raiders stir up the volatility of the market and thereby jack up the risk for all the participants. In these ways, the spree of predation results in a negative sum game for the population as a whole.

Given this backdrop, the band of market scalpers resembles the herd of hedge funds in a number of ways. For each type of operator, the baneful outcomes include the cutdown of efficiency and the crank-up of turbulence in the market.

By piling in and out of the bazaar en masse, the bettors in the hedge fund game pump up the volatility in the forum. Meanwhile, the asset bubbles that ensue serve to foul up the allocation of resources in the financial ring as well as the real economy.

The distortions can be so severe that the bust of a bubble ends up knocking down the financial system as well as the larger economy. A fine example lay in the blowup of 2008 along with the global recession in its wake.

As the catastrophe unfolded, the general public was largely unaware of the full scope of the damage to their wealth and well-being. The smashup in fact amounted to many trillions of dollars in each of the major countries of the world. The cost of cleaning up the mess, as well as the loss of productive output in the global economy, each added up to trillions more.

Throughout the debacle and its aftermath, the financial media provided scant information on the true extent of the damage to investors as well as consumers. Despite the shortage of hard facts, though, the populace was astute enough to recognize the need for sweeping changes and to demand concerted action by the government.

Over the next couple of years, elected officials round the world made a big show of denouncing the culprits behind the calamity. The targets in their sights included hedge funds bulked up by mindless amounts of leverage as well as commercial banks that flogged flaky products while deceiving their customers.

The hailstorm of anger and disgust raging through the electorate provided the political class with a golden opportunity to clear the decks and start over with a clean slate of financial legislation. In the end, though, the policymakers largely squandered the gift of political capital.

If the lawmakers had acted boldly and decisively, they could have torn down the rickety house of finance and put up a robust structure in its stead. In the process, the politicos would have served the common weal and – better yet from their perspective – earned gobs of Brownie points amongst their constituents. Yet that was not to be.

Instead, the pols huffed and puffed but ended up with little to show for all the sound and fury. On one hand, the vote mongers did make a hopeful start in the aftershock of the blowup. The politicos began with loud noises about drumming up a fresh batch of laws to usher in a brand-new era of virtue, stability and prosperity.

On the other hand, it soon became clear to everyone that the bluster was mostly a blast of hot air. Right after the wimpy bills passed into law, even the pols themselves gave up the tinny claims of ringing in radical reforms. In the end, the pols merely managed to slap a few bandages here and there upon the blighted corpus of finance.

Put another way, the slapdash remedies fixed up by the lawmakers merely dabbled around the edges and left untouched the seeds of the malaise. As a result, the financial forum as well as the real economy were left to suffer from flare-ups of equal – or more likely, greater – severity in due course.

Given the shortage of foresight and gumption, bigger bombshells will have to explode before the lawmakers work up the courage to deal with the threat in a serious way. From the depths of the crises to erupt in the future, an obvious point of departure is to stamp out the welter of schemes that destroy wealth and aggravate risk in the entire populace.

As it always was, so it is today: what the world needs is a few good statesmen to step into the void and take up the cause on behalf of the society at large. At stake is the integrity of the financial markets along with the security of the investing public. An even bigger issue lies in the stability of the real economy along with the welfare of the entire population of producers and consumers.

As we saw earlier, the financial forum as a whole is a positive sum game. Yet there are toxic patches in the landscape, along with a few clumps of corrosive elements, which give rise to negative payoffs.

The investing public would stand to benefit greatly if the schemes of the baneful kind were to be stamped out. The purge of shell games would also bolster the effectiveness of the stock market as an institution; and likewise for the other branches of the financial system. The healthful change would also help to beef up the chains of production and distribution, with positive results for all the participants in the economy at large.

Wrap-up of High Frequency Trading

At the dawn of the millennium, the robotic agent engaged in high frequency trading has been replacing the human trader as the dominant actor in electronic markets. According to received wisdom, an increase in trading volume shores up the liquidity in the market and thereby pares down the cost of transactions for all the participants.

This type of argument was valid in the olden days when human beings bought and sold assets using manual procedures. Moreover, the logic held sway – and applies even today – when live players make independent decisions while relegating computer systems to a secondary role. The ancillary functions of a digital aide include the passive collection of facts, the graphic display of data, and the prompt dispatch of orders.

On the other hand, the situation is entirely different when software agents are deployed in a predatory mode. The schemes of the latter type include the dispatch of flash orders as a way to extract information from the investing public in an underhanded way. A related move is the purchase and sale of securities in bulk in order to corner the market. By yanking the prices around, the raiders transform the smooth changes in the marketplace into sudden jerks.

In this setting, the benefits of high turnover are turned upside down as the software agents prosecute a campaign of high frequency trading. The traders of this breed do not bother to analyze the value of a stock or even digest the historical record of transactions.

Rather, the virtual drones probe the market to figure out which way the investing public is moving. Then the upstarts dash in front of the crowd with the aim of manipulating the market on a fleeting basis for a quick profit.

A direct impact of the bushwhack is a hike in the cost of transactions for the investing public. To compound the drubbing, the market pitches up and down with bigger hops than it would in the absence of manipulation. The immediate consequence is to crank up the volatility and cut down the stability of the financial forum.

In these ways, the market as a whole suffers from the onslaught of the robotic scalpers. The baleful impact of algo trading is a cutdown of profit coupled with an upsurge of risk for the genuine investor in tandem with the financial community at large.

Chapter 8

Curbing the Carnage

As we have seen, the throng of hedge funds poses a serious threat to the investing public as well as the financial system and the real economy. In the absence of radical change, the horde of wildcats will continue to run amok and wreak havoc in the marketplace.

The menace goes far deeper than the general public – including investors, policymakers and commentators – has recognized thus far. Under the existing lineup of reward and punishment, sheer logic in tandem with a basic grasp of human nature dictates that hedge funds will assault the marketplace with increasing violence as time goes by.

Unless the matchup of gain and pain were to change, the operators will continue to take on absurd amounts of risk. The sword of Damocles is set to set to deliver a mortal blow to the financial system as well as the larger economy.

For the clients of hedge funds, the proposition is in essence the same as buying a lottery ticket or playing the casino. A few punters might win big on occasion, but the bettors in the aggregate are doomed to lose time and time again. The only players who win consistently are the operators of the games.

Social Benefits of a Lottery

A public lottery happens to be a juicy deal for the government. As a rule, the sponsoring agency hives off 50 to 80 percent of the gross receipts and funnels the windfall into the public treasury. The remainder of the proceeds is paid out to the participants in the form of prizes to a few winners.

In the United States, a representative figure is a payout rate of one-third of the intake.[38] Put another way, the players on average receive 33 cents on each dollar they put into the pot at the outset.

On the upside, the public lottery has a redeeming streak in that the lion's share of the profit is plowed back into the local community. As an example, many programs run by state agencies in the U.S. use a big chunk of the bounty to shore up the educational system.

The pedagogical thrust of the program seems highly fitting. The bulk of lottery tickets are purchased by bettors in the lower income brackets. Moreover, the educational level of the clientele tends to be lower than that of the population at large. As a result, the lottery system is known in some quarters as a "tax on stupidity".

If the bettors were to receive a better education, they would presumably wean themselves of the habit due to the odds stacked against them. With a clear head, the punters would be in better shape to fend off the urge to gamble and fritter away their meager coin on a losing proposition.

Although no one likes to talk about it, the situation is similar when it comes to the hedge fund game. The main difference is that the latter scheme can only be marketed to affluent customers who supposedly can afford to lose a lot of money.

The second crucial distinction is that the profits from the operation go mainly to the individuals who run the games. The arrangement is a far cry from the shunting of profits to the public purse as the prime beneficiary of a state lottery.

A third hallmark involves the fact that hedge funds as a group take up extremely risky bets, including the positions propped up by levered schemes. As a result, the plungers have an impact on the marketplace far beyond the stash of capital entrusted to them by the investors.

A direct corollary is a distortion of demand for the assets that happen to be in vogue, along with the resulting warpage of prices. The mutilation of price signals in the marketplace gives rise to the misallocation of the factors of production. The upshot is a waste of scads of resources.

A prime example lay in the mindless uptake of financial derivatives based on risky mortgages at the dawn of the millennium. The levered ploy by the rabid players – in the form of reckless groups at investment banks, insurance firms, and boutique outfits – stood upon a heap of rickety assets.

The financial rigs were molded out of bits and pieces of risky loans issued to borrowers of all stripes. Many of the debtors standing behind the loans had flimsy credit ratings or even none at all.

To make matters worse, the mortagages were sliced and diced, then mashed and wrapped using a welter of convoluted schemes. The resulting packets were so jumbled and complex that no one could understand the true nature of their properties or their subsequent performance in the marketplace.

Despite an army of staff members armed with advanced degrees and analytic tools, the fabricators themselves could not in all honesty claim to grasp the behavior of the Frankenstein blobs under various conditions over time. In that case, it was unreasonable to suppose that the mass of customers, observers, or anyone else could plumb the destructive power of the ill-conceived products.

House of Cards

Thanks to a ready market for flaky products in the financial bazaar, a host of commercial banks gleefully churned out the building blocks by the truckload. Amid the gold rush, zealous lenders managed to cajole millions of prospects – including the penniless and the jobless – to take on massive amounts of mortgages.

In many cases, the banksters were eager to sign up unwitting customers who were in no shape to service the debt over the long range. The problem for the debtors lay in the inevitable rise of interest rates in the years to follow.

The feeding frenzy in real estate had begun as the central bank slashed the basic rate of interest to abnormally low levels. The purpose of the loose policy was to pull the economy out of the recession sparked by the blowup of the Internet bubble.

As a rule, a recession in the modern era lasts only a couple of quarters. In that case, anyone with a passing knowledge of the real world in general or the housing market in particular would be aware of the obvious: the interest rate would begin to rise as soon as the economy gave off some credible signs of stirring back to life.

When the interest rate clambers upward, so does the size of the installment payments on the mortgages marked to adjustable rates. Clearly, anyone on a strained budget would be unable to keep up with the mounting burden.

Rigging a Bombshell

Without the means to service the growing load of payments, legions of homeowners would have to surrender their properties to the banksters. In fact, even borrowers with decent credit ratings would struggle to keep up with the swelling millstone of monthly payments.

The resulting barrage of defaults and foreclosures would plainly lead to a cataclysm for everyone caught up in the flaky scheme as well as the innocents watching in horror from the sidelines. Sooner or later, the crackup of the housing bubble would obliterate wealth on a humongous scale.

The specter of default on the mortgages was not a vague possibility, but an assured outcome. It's common knowledge that the cost of borrowing rises *when* – rather than *if* – the central bank restores the basic rate of interest to normal levels after a spell of unusually low rates.

In the throes of the lending spree, the insatiable demand for real estate fueled a frenzy of construction in the housing sector. The turnout was a market chockablock with properties that had no other function than serving as vessels for speculation.

In many countries round the world, ranging from the U.S. and Britain to Spain and Latvia, berserk buyers bid up the price of real estate far beyond the bounds of sanity. When the bubble burst, the aftershock could only be calamitous.

The climax was the financial crisis of 2008. The blowout gave rise to the worst debacle since the Great Depression of the 1930s.

So severe was the smashup in the stock market and the banking system that the real economy plunged into a tailspin as well. The upshot was the grimmest recession the world had known since the devastation of World War II.

So Much for So Many Bashed So Fast by So Few

Amid the catastrophe, it was not only the throng of investors that lost their nest eggs when the hedgies large and small blew up by the thousands. Rather, the larger population of consumers and producers paid the price for the misbegotten schemes.

One direct fallout was the cutdown of trillions of dollars in each of the stock markets of note round the world. Another outcome was the loss of trillions of dollars in output as the global economy tumbled into the Great Recession.

On one hand, hard statistics on the calamity are hard to come by on a worldwide basis. Even so, we can get some idea of the enormity of the wipeout by looking at the experience of the United States.

In that country alone, household wealth tumbled by 18%, amounting to $12 trillion, between 2007 and 2010.[39] The takedown can be traced mainly to the collapse of the stock market and the housing sector.

The preceding estimate of the drubbing entailed does not take into account the damage due to the jobs destroyed and the output foregone. The recession would in fact vaporize trillions of dollars in the making due to the squelch of economic activity during and after the financial flap.

Primed for Regret

A fourth bane of rampant speculation crops up in the aftermath of the blowup. In a frantic search for easy answers, the government resorts to the batty practice of using public funds to rescue the pillagers from their own follies.

A stark example lay in the redemption of an insurance firm named American International Group (AIG) as it broke down in the aftershock of the financial blowup. As the skewered giant keeled over, the government stepped forth and propped up the insurer to the tune of $182.5 billion. Yet it was sheer fantasy to think that the money was used wisely.

To add insult to injury, the executives at AIG used part of the cash infusion to line their own pockets. As an example, a swag of $165 million in bonuses[40] was doled out in spring 2009 to the jokers within the very gang responsible for wrecking the company in the first place!

This sort of floozy behavior was not what the American taxpayer had signed up for. Nor was it the intent of Uncle Sam in handing out the bailout funds to the ravaged firm.

The incident was a fine example of the nutty practice of rewarding precisely the wrong characters in the wake of a catastrophe. Sadly, though, the perverse course of action has to date been the norm rather than the exception in public policy.

Looking at the larger picture, the problem is not just a matter of wasting mounds of wealth in order to reward a bunch of gamblers who trashed a huge pile of money and wrecked their own company. Rather, the predicament happens to be more fundamental: the custom of raiding the public treasury for billions of dollars at a time, and trillions of bucks in the aggregate, in order to reverse a bunch of private failures.

Simply put, the operators of hedge funds get to keep a large chunk of the spoils when their bets work out while the investors and taxpayers end up footing the bill when the schemes go sour. And, there's worse news still. Unhappily, the nutty practice of privatizing the profits and socializing the costs is only part of the tawdry tale.

As we noted earlier, a spree of speculation on steroids – pumped up by the use of other people's money – leads to gross distortions in the marketplace. The warpage of prices in turn gives rise to the perverted allocation of assets. The resources in the latter category take the form of capital, labor and materiel.

While the feeding frenzy is in full swing, a direct impact is the cutout of useful production in the real economy due to the diversion of resources into wasteful schemes. Further down the line, another dire outcome is the wholesale rubout of wealth when the bonfire of greed runs out of feedstock and the blaze peters out.

As the bubble implodes, the aftershock clobbers not only the plungers at center stage, but the investors watching from the sidelines. All too often, the entire population suffers from the fallout as the economy at large tumbles into a crippling recession.

Trail of Destruction

To sum up, hedge funds as a group are wreckers in disguise rather than the builders of wealth imagined by the investing public. First of all, in-depth studies have shown that the outfits turn in *gross* returns which are *negative* after accounting for the biases in sampling due to survivorship, self-selection and the like.

Secondly, the *net* returns to the customers are even worse for a number of reasons. The main reason for the ravage stems from the performance fees by which the operators take a cut – usually ranging from 20 to 50 percent – of the windfall after any spell in which the portfolio happens to show a profit beyond its prior peak.

Another source of dissipation lies in the couple of percent hived off each year in the form of maintenance fees. The administrative load is levied against the pool regardless of the performance of the portfolio.

Yet another reason for the underperformance can be traced to the grind of transaction fees incurred by the frenetic schedule of trading. The turnover of assets by hedge funds is roughly twice the level for the regulated pools in the form of mutual funds. As a result, the bleeding rate for the hedgies would be about twice as great.

Thirdly, the extreme levels of leverage used on dicey ploys leads to a rash of noxious effects. A case in point is the mangling of prices in the marketplace in favor of assets whose main function is to serve as tools of speculation for gamblers rather than objects of value for investors.

During the build-up of a bubble, the surge in price sucks in a mass of resources in the form of capital, labor and materiel. If the price signals had not been loused up, the factors of production could have been put to worthwhile uses rather than frittered away on flippant schemes.

Another bugbear involves the crushing impact of the aftershock when the bubble pops, as it is wont to do sooner or later. The grisly effects include the mauling of the financial forum as well as the banking system. The rampage in turn pummels hale firms as well as frail concerns in the real economy.

Another byproduct is the squelch of wealth to the tune of trillions of dollars in the financial markets. The rubout of virtual assets is accompanied by a blowout on a comparable scale for tangible products; namely, the heaps of output foregone when the economy tumbles into a recession.

Other setbacks include the expenditure of trillions of dollars by the governments of the world in a frantic attempt to revive their lifeless economies. Sadly, the flurry of makeshift programs cobbled together in haste usually turns out to be wasteful in the short run. Worse yet, the whirlwind of activity is often feckless and even counterproductive over the long range.

In the autumn of the 20th century, when concrete information on hedge funds was scanty or nonexistent, the scheme was defended by the claim that the custodians were skilled in the arts of investment. According to the party line, a cadre of full-time professionals could generate higher returns on average than the amateurs on the periphery. The outsiders in the latter category would span the gamut from individual investors and commercial creditors to pension funds and sovereign pools.

In flogging this line of argument, the defenders of course glossed over the fact that a cockeyed set of incentives dangled in front of the operators. Apparently, the custodians were benign angels who would work against their own interests in order to safeguard the welfare of their customers.

Since that jejune era, however, a series of detailed studies by impartial probers has shown up the fallacy of the popular myth. To begin with, hedge funds in the aggregate trail behind the benchmarks of the market even before taking into account the losses for the investors due to maintenance charges and other factors. In fact, the stewards actually manage to destroy wealth for their clients. The performance of hedge funds as a group happens to be much lower than the turnout for a pile of inert cash tucked under a mattress.

To compound the problem, the hounds in the hedge fund game rush in and out of the market en masse as they chase after the latest fads. The inevitable outturn is to pump up the volatility of the market and thus cut down the risk-to-reward ratio for all the participants in the forum.

Another doleful effect is the impact on the real economy whenever a frenzy expands to loony proportions. When a bubble of grotesque size blows up, the entire economy plunges into a recession. The aftershock cuts down millions of jobs and wipes out trillions of dollars in every major country round the world.

In the final analysis, the swarm of hedge funds is a destroyer of wealth rather than the creator of riches imagined by the general public. The spree of havoc beats up the larger population of investors, creditors and other stakeholders.

The same is true of the algo trader whose goal is to waylay the investing public and commandeer the economic surplus in the market. The war of attrition against the investing public does not merely transfer money from one party to another, but is in fact a wasteful scheme that shrinks the overall trove of wealth available to the entire community. Put another way, the maneuver is not a zero sum game but a gimmick that yields a negative score.

The campaign of bushwhacking by the scalpers, along with the program of demolition by the hedgies, hobbles the efficiency of the market and sets the stage for blowups on a devastating scale. The resulting smackdown of the real economy then clobbers the entire population of investors and creditors, consumers and producers, companies and institutions.

Armed to the teeth with weapons of mass destruction, the army of hedge funds can cut a brutish path through the marketplace. Propped up by tools of gross leverage, the throng of wildcats can also punch far above their weight.

At the microlevel of the individual as well as the macrolevel of the economy, the impact on the society at large turns out to be profoundly negative.

Chapter 9

A Wholesome Remedy

Given the plethora of ills associated with hedge funds, it would be short-sighted to leave things the way they are or to simply tinker round the edges. A bumbling response of this sort will simply sow the seeds of future bombshells whose blowups are apt to be worse than all those that have gone before.

To follow up on the previous chapter, one way to approach the task of reform is to begin with the similarities and differences between hedge funds and state lotteries. In particular, a public program of sweepstakes boasts a number of wholesome traits that could be carried over into the vale of hedge funds.

During the first half of the 20th century, lotteries were illegal in many countries. Only after World War II did governments show a serious interest in using the scheme as a way to shore up the public treasury.

In the U.S., for instance, the first lottery of the modern era was set up in New Hampshire in 1964. By 2008, though, just about every state in the country had followed suit.

The widespread uptake, along with the fruitful outcome, of this policy set the stage for a straightforward way to deal with the bogey of hedge funds. The answer is to get rid of private schemes and turn over the business to public agencies.

Direct Ownership by the Government

When the public sector gets involved, the government may or may not run the programs on a workaday basis. Rather than handling the operations directly, the main idea is to assume overall responsibility for the programs.

In that case, each pool would be sponsored by a public agency. As an example, the government might own 90% of the common stock in a hedge fund which is structured as a public corporation and listed on a stock exchange. The remaining 10% of the shares would be available for trading on the bourse.

The main reason for the partial flotation of stock is to facilitate the valuation of the outfit. The reaction of the investing public to the equity would serve as a yardstick for comparison amongst kindred pools. The same is true in sizing up the fund against the performance of unrelated firms in diverse branches of the stock market.

For instance, a hedge fund with a price-to-earnings ratio that exceeds the average level on the bourse would be rated favorably. In that case, the managers of the hedge fund might be entitled to an extra bonus.

Defending the Financial System

A big advantage of direct ownership by the government stems from the confidence of the investing public along with the stability of the financial system. Even in the absence of an official guarantee, investors would be less prone to get hysterical when a particular pool blows up or even the entire bourse breaks down.

Moreover, the wipeout of one or more outfits owned largely by the government would not threaten to destroy the entire meshwork of finance in the local economy nor the global marketplace. Under the traditional scheme, the collapse of a single firm has the punch to bring down the whole shebang.

In fact, the specter of a chain reaction has been invoked numerous times in the past in order to justify hasty programs of direct intervention by the government. A glaring example involved the smashup of a hedge fund that was launched in 1994.

Bungling Moves

In spite of its name – Long-Term Capital Management – the outfit had scant interest in investing for the long range. Thanks to a shallow grasp of the marketplace coupled with a massive load of leverage, LTCM managed to lose $4.6 billion within a span of four months in 1998.

The bombshell shattered more than the hedge fund itself. In fact, the explosion was set to knock out a posse of big banks that had lent the plunger scads of money in order to take up mounds of levered bets.

Amid the threat of a system-wide collapse, the central bank had to step in and orchestrate a bailout package amounting to $3.6 billion.[41] In the end, the infusion of capital could not save the hedge fund itself, which died a couple of years later from its self-inflicted wounds. On the other hand, the rescue package did stave off a chain reaction of blowups in the financial sector.

In dealing with crises that rarely crop up, it might make sense for the government to sit on its haunches and wait until a calamity pops up before springing into action. On the other hand, the laid-back policy is a clumsy and costly approach when man-made flaps flare up with increasing frequency and severity.

Amid the financial crisis of 2008, for instance, the loss of trillions of dollars by investors, producers and consumers in every major country around the globe was baleful enough. Grim as it was, though, the mayhem in plain sight revealed only part of the whole picture.

The common consensus among experts was that the catastrophe could easily have turned out to be far worse. In fact, the carnage that ensued might have matched or surpassed the holocaust of the Great Depression. The latter debacle of course paved the way the holocaust of the Second World War.

When the threat is big enough, it makes good sense to take an active approach to prevent a replay in the future. Where hedge funds are concerned, there are several ways to clean up the act.

Boons of Ownership

As we noted earlier, one way to contain the threat is to place the ownership of the pools in the hands of the government. This approach offers a medley of advantages.

One kind of allure lies in the direct benefits to be gained. The obvious draw lies in the shunting of profits into the public treasury. Another benefit is an increase in transparency for the investors and other stakeholders, along with the information needed to make clear-headed decisions.

A second type of benefit takes the form of indirect gains. In line with earlier remarks, the ownership in part or in whole by the government will doubtless bolster the confidence of the investing public. The implicit guarantee of stability will help to quell any panics that crop up when a particular fund breaks down or the entire market keels over.

Licensing for a Select Group of Pacers

Another way to curb the threat of hedge funds is to give out permits to a small group of accomplished players in the private sector. An example of the latter is a private outfit with a long history of superior performance based on a stable program of trading while relying solely on internal funds.

In sizing up the candidates, the crucial feature is the average return adjusted for risk. In particular, the portfolio ought to be less volatile than a comparable index of the market in order to deserve its label as a *hedge* fund rather than a gambling pool.

Moreover, the candidate should have no skeletons in the closet. A counterexample involves a pillager dogged by a bloody trail of bludgeoned portfolios that were beaten to a pulp and buried quietly out of view of the investing public.

Under the licensing approach, a small flock of high flyers would receive the go-ahead to offer their shares to the general public. In the interest of transparency, each hedge fund would be converted into a public corporation and listed on a stock exchange.

By contrast to a program of ownership, the government would have little or no stake in the equity of a licensed outfit. Instead, the shares would lie mostly in the hands of the investing public. The latter would then enjoy the bulk of any windfall generated by the pool.

The two types of programs described above are independent rather than exclusionary. As an example, the permitting approach may be implemented on its own as a stand-alone scheme. On the other hand, the program could also run in parallel with the ownership setup described earlier.

Either of the foregoing approaches would offer a host of advantages. For instance, a program of ownership by the government would serve to funnel the profits into the public coffers. In that case, the windfall could be spent on worthy causes such as beefing up the educational system.

Gambling with Other People's Money

It's no mystery why the operators of hedge funds take on heedless amounts of risk even at the cost of wrecking their own firms as a result. The reason is that the stewards can help themselves to a fat share of the profits on an upswing while they foot none of the losses on the downstroke. The bettors have a lot to gain, and nothing to lose, by going out on a limb.

Given this backdrop, a simple way to curb the glut of speculation in the bazaar is to ban the use of other people's money for rickety schemes. More precisely, an operator should not have access to leverage, nor control a stake beyond the equity embodied by the assets under management. The ploys of the forbidden kind include loans from commercial banks as well as tools such as financial derivatives.

Clearly, the foregoing policy would not preclude the use of financial instruments across the board. As a counterexample, an operator would be free to buy a contract in the futures market if the notional value of the assets controlled by the position were less than the net worth of the portfolio at hand.

In addition, the stricture against leverage would exclude players that do not rely on other people's money. To be precise, a speculator would be free to take on as much risk as their heart desires should they choose to gamble only with their own purse. *When* – rather than *if* – the risky scheme blows up, the damage would be borne solely by the reckless bettor.

In that case, the throng of blameless parties standing on the sidelines would for the most part be protected from the aftershock. The innocents of this stripe include investors in the financial forum as well as consumers in the real economy.

Admittedly, the market as a whole could quake if a lot of bettors were to go bust at the same time. Even so, the damage would be confined largely to the participants having direct exposure to the marketplace.

In that case, the financial system as a whole would be saved from the systemic crackup sparked by a chain reaction of bankruptcies amongst the reckless players and their backers. Moreover, the real economy would be spared the usual abuse in the wake of a massive blowup in the financial bazaar.

To round up, there's no need to expose the entire community of investors, consumers and producers to the bombshells set off by a small pack of wildcats. For practical reasons as well as moral grounds, the innocents in the world at large should not have to pay for the follies of the bettors that play fast and loose with other people's savings.

Chapter 10

Light in the Dark

Since the twilight of the 20th century, a series of rigorous studies has exposed the truth behind the popular image of hedge funds as savvy traders. After correcting for a variety of errors due to biased sampling, the gross returns not come close to matching the benchmarks of the market in terms of either risk or payoff. The performance is of course even worse in terms of risk-adjusted returns.

Naturally, the net impact on the customers is still worse for a number of reasons. An example lies in the incessant grind of maintenance fees regardless of the outcome for the portfolio. Another sample is the burden of full liability for any losses incurred by the operators.

Given this backdrop, why do myriads of investors clamor for the jerry-built rigs in spite of the cruddy results on offer? The only plausible answer is that the prospects are largely unaware of the reality behind the facade.

In that case, it makes sense to educate the investing public about the true nature of the hedge fund game. To this end, an obvious point of departure is a trenchant program of information and counsel sponsored in whole or in part by public agencies.

As an example, the government could establish an online portal to improve the financial literacy of the investing public. Admittedly, a number of hubs on the Internet have taken a few token steps in this direction.

A case in point is a notice tucked away in the cellars of the Web site maintained by the U.S. Securities and Exchange Commission. The posting advises investors to guard against an outbreak of outright fraud in the financial markets.

The investing public is urged to conduct their own due diligence. On the other hand, the site provides practically no information needed by the investor in order to do their homework in a serious way.

On a positive note, an obscure alert by a government watchdog – skimpy though it be – has got to be better than nothing at all from a moral standpoint. Even so, it seems fair to say that there is plenty of room for improvement.

Owing to the shortage of materials, the hapless investor is hard-pressed to find any type of meaty information – aside perhaps from the cursory reports filed by the companies themselves.

Given the dearth of resources, the public sector ought to step up and fill in the void. More precisely, government should set up a coherent hub designed to support investors, journalists and other interested parties.

The Web site would serve up a smorgasbord of helpful content in an engaging style. The resources should provide a sturdy foundation for all types of visitors, including the investors drawn to hedge funds or other unstable schemes.

As a point of departure, the educational site could offer basic information on crucial issues for the investor to mull over. A showcase of this sort involves a lineup of articles on the linkage between risk and return for different classes of investment vehicles.

Another type of resource is a gallery of user-friendly videos on the false image of profits cooked up by patchy statistics. A case in point is the unreal estimate of performance in the hedge fund game due to the severe bias caused by high mortality, low survivorship, and other knotty factors.

Armageddon in the Marketplace

For the starring role they played in knocking down the financial system and the real economy, hedge funds staggered into the public limelight in the autumn of 2008. Admittedly, the wildcats were not the only actors on the scene by any means. Even so, the artists took center stage and dominated the plot as it thickened and ruptured.

In the run-up to the blowup, a frenzy in real estate had been brewing for years thanks in large measure to the craving for risky assets by the speculators in the financial bazaar. The resulting groundswell of prices led in turn to a cascade of dislocations in the real economy.

Under normal circumstances, the inevitable bust of the bubble would have prompted a garden-variety recession like so many others in the past. This time, though, the tangible economy as well as the financial system were not as fortunate. Due to the colossal pileup of speculation and leverage prior to the climax, the blowout led to the worst fallout in more than half a century.

The fiasco proved in a spectacular way that a house of cards built on leverage can cause a chain reaction on a whopping scale. The end result was to lay waste to the capital markets as well as the banking system and the real economy.

In the wake of the disaster, the general public clamored for the government to take concrete action to avert such crackups in the future. Sadly, though, the policymakers drew the wrong conclusions from the crisis and resorted in their usual fashion to a grab bag of easy answers.

To begin with, the corps of elected officials failed to grasp the entire chain of causality behind the bombshell. Moreover, the lawmakers wanted to believe that a makeshift balm would be enough to repress the threat.

With this mindset, the implausible cure was drummed up amid great clangor and passed into law with huge fanfare. While the brew might have looked appealing to some folks, the concoction did not come close to stamping out the threat for real.

If wishes were balms, then migraines would vanish. Sadly, though, flicking a few dabs of ointment on a decrepit critter is not enough to transform the beast. Needless to say, a facile move of this sort would merely open the door to future outbursts.

To dispatch the ailment for good, the remedy has to wipe out the scourge by the roots. A sweeping program of treatment is needed in order to cure the disease rather than mask the syndrome.

Speculators as Looters or Scapegoats

When a nation staggers into a crisis of the financial or economic kind, a standard ploy of the political class is to distract the population by averting their gaze. For this purpose, a dandy ruse is to denounce some vague gang of speculators as the agent of misfortune.

A glaring example cropped up after the blowup of the local currency in Malaysia during the Asian crisis of 1997. Another instance was the breakdown of the bond market in Greece amid the European flap of 2010.

In each of these cases, the speculators in the wings were in truth the messengers rather than the ringleaders behind the fiasco. Prior to either bombshell, the financial bazaar had been severely out of whack with the real economy.

More precisely, the tangible economy had been pumped up by a blizzard of rampant expenditures over the course of a decade and more. Much of the spree had in fact been orchestrated by the politicians, supported in large part by a troupe of heedless foreigners who were willing to foot the bill in the hope of bagging a windfall.

On the other hand, the outlay of vast sums of money for unproductive schemes set the stage for a painful denouement. An exemplar lay in the headlong construction of commercial properties, or the manic handout of subsidies to appease the voters. In this unhealthy setting, the financial forum as well as the real economy would have broken down at some point whether or not any speculators had been involved.

Moreover, the sudden flight of capital from each of the beleaguered nations could be ascribed mostly to the jitters of the investing public rather than the machinations of evil speculators. The fearful players in the forum scrounged up whatever cash they could on short notice, then sent off the money for safekeeping in safe havens abroad. The gamesters of this breed included long-term investors in the global marketplace as well as wealthy citizens within the battered country.

On their own, a gaggle of speculators has scant power to destroy the financial system or the tangible economy across an entire country, let alone the whole world. In fact, many have argued – with good cause in some cases – that speculators tend to improve the efficiency of the marketplace by upping the volume of transactions.

As a rule, an increase in turnover adds to the liquidity in the forum. The upswell can at times reduce the cost of interaction as well as lubricate the wheels of finance and commerce.

For an enterprise in the real economy, the benefits of liquidity are reflected in the ease of raising capital through the sale of stock to the general public. In a similar way, a private investor can buy or sell a security with less friction than otherwise.

As a result, a speculator can streamline the flow of funds in the financial bazaar. The fruitful turnout helps to boost the vitality of the real economy as well.

For these reasons, speculation per se is not the problem. Nor is leverage in itself a universal threat. Rather, the real bogey lies in speculation and leverage of the inane kind.

On one hand, a modicum of gearing in support of business activity can be beneficial to a company as well as the economy at large. On the other hand, an excess of leverage is nothing more than a front for playing the sweepstakes.

To add to the muddle, the dicey schemes are prosecuted under the fanciful name of "investment" rather than the gambling that it really is. For a number of reasons, then, a lot of folks have been unable to recognize the difference between leverage of the benign and malignant kinds.

Use and Misuse of Leverage

As in the case of speculation, a dollop of leverage can be useful for workaday commerce. For a simple example, we turn to the automobile industry.

It makes sense for a carmaker to safeguard its profits from the vagaries of exchange rates in a global marketplace. After all, the company's forte lies in making cars rather than trading currencies.

For this type of concern, there's no practical way to obtain adequate protection without the use of a levered position. More precisely, a small kitty has to serve as the collateral in controlling a position large enough to fully cover the expected earnings from foreign markets.

As an example, a carmaker based in the U.S. might *sell* a futures contract on the euro in order to shelter the firm's profits earned in the European market. Due to the inverse position of having sold rather than bought the contract, a fall in the value of the euro will result in a gain for the company.

If the currency in Europe were to slump, the value of each euro would be lower than before when the earnings are converted into dollars. On the other hand, the comedown of the currency itself will be offset by the profit – to a greater or lesser degree – due to the sale of the futures contract. In this way, any turmoil in the currency market can be countered by an opposing move in the futures market.

From a pragmatic stance, the levered position in the futures market is taken up as a counterweight to the inflow of hard cash expected from the commercial business. For this reason, the uptake of the futures contract is said to be a *covered* position.

On the other hand, the problems crop up when a levered ploy serves no useful function in the real economy. To make matters worse, the leverage is often pumped up far beyond the bounds of reason in the fond hope of hitting the jackpot.

In fact, the positions are often so precarious that a fleeting blip – let alone a cyclic wave or a secular trend – can wipe out the entire portfolio containing the levered stake. A case in point is a plunger that takes up leverage amounting to 50 times the entire equity in the trading account.

In that case, a ripple of just 2 percent in the price of the target asset will wipe out the account completely. Moreover, once the value of the account hits zero, the portfolio is dead and gone forever.

Granted, a tenacious player could put more money into the account and fire up the program of trading once more. On the other hand, the fresh infusion of cash does nothing to restore the capital that has been obliterated. The account number might be the same, but the newborn pool represents a completely different game altogether.

A twitch in price of a couple of percent happens to be a routine event even in a market of modest volatility. An example of this sort lies in stocks or currencies. In certain fields such as options or futures, jumps of far greater size occur as a matter of course.

In many cases, witless traders take up levered positions that crank up the bets by a factor of 100 or more. Not surprisingly, the gamblers of this breed bite the dust in droves when the market hits a rough patch, as it's bound to do sooner or later.

Given the plethora of turbocharged tools in the financial forum, a punter can easily jack up the leverage from a puny base of capital. To make matters worse, the mountain of risk can be stacked even higher by rounding up cash from wealthy investors or setting up lines of credit from commercial banks.

Warped Prices and Twisted Markets

To exacerbate the problem, the surfeit of leverage creates an artificial demand for the assets in vogue. The objects in the latter category may take the form of stocks, commodities or any other goods. The resulting surge in price attracts even more plungers into the arena, thus turning a flaming bonfire into a raging inferno.

An exemplar lay in the ravenous demand for mortgage-based assets during the run-up to the financial crisis of 2008. The craving for high-yield debt on Wall Street prompted a horde of commercial lenders on Main Street to issue mounds of risky mortgages.

So reckless was the binge of lending by the banksters that borrowers of all stripes, including the jobless and the destitute, were often cajoled into taking on multiple mortgages for houses that would stand empty for want of tenants. To cap it all off, the debt mongers also handed out loans for use as down-payments on lavish properties that never amounted to anything more than fanciful sketches on a drawing board.

The gush of loose money in real estate could not help but lead to surging prices. The groundswell of demand in the housing sector in turn brought out a welter of physical stock that had no practical use other than serving as vehicles for speculation.

This vignette spotlights the fact that uncontrolled betting propped up by external sources of funding gives rise to swollen prices, which in turn wrenches the market out of shape. In this way, the warpage induced by the binge of speculation prior to the bombshell is the real cause of the mayhem that ensues.

Given this backdrop, the sensible way to cure the malady is to put a lid on rampant speculation from the get-go. In this way, the germs of the disease can be stamped out rather than the syndrome merely papered over.

Forces of Good and Evil

A standard way to highlight a concept in any domain is to coin a brand-new term. For this purpose, the neologism could rely on a word in everyday language.

For a simple example, we turn to the natural sciences. The term *energy* is defined by the physicist in a constrained way that differs markedly from the broad meaning of the word in daily life.

On the other hand, a newborn term could also be minted from scratch. A case in point is the word *blockbuster*, which sprang to life in the 1940s.

To date, though, there has been no terminology in common use to distinguish between harmful and benign forms of speculation. The deficit stems from the fact that the financial community – ranging from professional traders and amateur investors to academic researchers and market watchers – has a habit of glossing over any distinctions between the constructive and destructive types of betting.

In fact, the bulk of the participants and commentators in the marketplace do not even realize that there is any meaningful difference between one mode of betting versus another. To most people, the whole ragbag of arcane schemes for speculation and leverage is a baffling mess that's best left untouched and unexamined.

Unfortunately, it's the widespread neglect by the larger community that allows the lethal forms of betting to run wild and wreak havoc on the financial system as well as the real economy. As a basic step toward redressing the problem, we will introduce a handful of suitable terms.

Hawkish versus Dovish Hedging

For the example of the carmaker we saw earlier, the firm hedged its exposure to the currency market in order to protect its earnings from the turmoil of exchange rates. This type of maneuver may be classified as a *defensive* form of hedging.

To be precise, the exposure to the currency market due to the futures contract is countered by the stream of earnings resulting from the business activities. In this way, the defensive hedge cuts down the risk faced by the company.

By contrast, a speculator takes on a surfeit of risk willingly in the hope of making a profit. A plain example is the purchase of a contract in the futures market backed only by the minimum amount of margin required by the futures exchange.

In the latter case, the trader is heavily exposed to the vicissitudes of the market. The futures contract is a *naked* position that is not backed by any asset which moves in the opposite direction.

For this reason, the gambit increases the risk of going bankrupt. The setup is the inverse of a hedged scheme whose aim is to counter any loss should the market move in an adverse fashion.

On the other hand, a naked position is not the only way to gain exposure to the market. Rather, a common practice for a speculator is to set up a hedge in a literal sense, but not in a meaningful way.

A case in point is the trader who buys a futures contract on crude oil and sells a corresponding instrument on natural gas. The dual position will show a net profit if the contract on oil were to outshine that for gas.

The reason for setting up the paired trade in the first place is to expose the speculator to the vagaries of the marketplace. If the punter wanted to avoid the risk of a wipeout, they could just have stayed away from the market entirely. Given this backdrop, the two-part gambit is an example of an *offensive* hedge.

In short, a hedge is not always what it seems at first glance. Certain tactics are consistent with the meaning of the word 'hedge' in that they reduce the risk of losing money. On the other hand, many a hedge belies the semantics and in fact inflates the odds of a catastrophic loss.

Safe versus Rash Leverage

As in the case of hedging, we can identify a couple of polar properties in connection with leverage. The key factor here involves the extent of the damage when the market takes a turn for the worse.

For the scenario of the futures market, suppose that the trader had placed only their own money at risk. Based on this gambit, the worst that could happen is that the punter would lose their own nest egg.

In that case, a breakdown of the portfolio will not directly whomp anyone else standing in the wings. For this reason, we may refer to the tactic as an example of *tame* or *internal* leverage.

By contrast, suppose that the trader had scrounged up a heap of money from external parties. For this purpose, the obvious modes of funding take the form of investments from customers or loans from banks.

In that case, the blowup that ensues will bash in the patrons in the wings as well as the operator at center stage. Due to the nasty impact on the passive stakeholders, we may refer to an overreaching move of this sort as *wild* or *external* leverage.

The financial flap of 2008 showed clearly that rampant leverage can bash in not only the active players in the market but knock down the entire meshwork of finance, banking and production. A striking feature of the debacle was the knockout of the banking system along with the rubout of credit for commercial firms in the real economy.

The smackdown of the financial infrastructure played a pivotal role in gutting the chains of production, distribution and consumption. Further down the line, the evisceration of the banking system hampered the frantic efforts of the government to pull the economy out of the Great Recession.

As the sources of credit dried up, even healthy firms were hard-pressed to obtain financing for routine operations such as shipping their products to foreign customers. The paralysis of the banks and the lack of funding dealt a body blow to companies both weak and strong. The knock-on effect was to aggravate the smackdown of the real economy caused by the carnage in the capital markets.

Given the scale of the catastrophe, it would make a good deal of sense to take concerted action to avert such blowups in the future. One of the steps in the right direction is to recognize the difference between one type of hedging versus another.

Even more crucial is the distinction between one mode of leverage versus another. The key to an effective program of safeguards is to stamp out hedging as well as gearing of the wild and lethal kinds.

Scant Leverage Causes Slight Hangover

The remarks above are not meant to suggest that leverage is the only way to cause a bubble. Plainly, a horde of independent investors acting on their own is perfectly capable of building up a bubble in the stock market, real estate, or any other domain.

An exemplar lay in the Internet craze of the late 1990s. In this case, the bubble sprang largely from the hype whipped up by gold diggers, zealous promoters, and private investors rather than the leverage drummed up by hedge funds, commercial banks, and the like.

On the other hand, lonesome players acting on their own are likely to hurt only themselves along perhaps with a small cadre of nearby neighbors. There's a good reason for the muted impact:

the bettors can scrape up so much money out of their own pockets and throw it on the bonfire before the feedstock runs out.

In that case, the resulting bombshell will be restricted for the most part to the participants puttering around the hotspot. For instance, a blowup of the stock market is apt to burn only investors while a breakdown of the housing sector is likely to bash only homeowners.

Admittedly, the aftershock could spread beyond its original turf to some extent. A case in point was the onset of a recession in the real economy after the Internet bubble popped in 2000.

On the other hand, the orgy of speculation will be milder in the absence of runaway leverage. In that case, the scope of the collateral damage will be constrained as well.

By contrast, the punters that use other people's money have practically boundless power to pump up a bubble. By driving up the price to batty heights, the gamesters can distort the market and thereby draw out a deluge of wasteful products.

A fine example lay in the pandemic of worthless ventures on the stock market during the Internet craze. Another sample was the sea of vacant homes amid the housing mania half a decade later.

In a nutshell, the use of other people's money for speculation results in the enthrallment of external parties. The victims caught in the snare range from private investors to commercial lenders. When – and not *if* – the bets go wrong and the plungers go bust, then their thralls on the sidelines suffer the brunt of the blowup.

In fact, the perverse matchup of gain and pain in the hedge fund game ensures that only the outsiders take the fall. In a parody of fairness and justice, the hustlers who caused the blowup get a free pass and walk away blithely without paying a pittance for the carnage that ensues.

The fiasco of 2008 proved without a shadow of doubt that a chain reaction sparked by a band of madcap players can bring down a slew of firms both healthy and sickly. Worse yet, the mayhem can be so severe as to knock down the capital markets, banking system, and the real economy on a worldwide basis.

To sum up, the use of external funds gives rabid speculators unlimited power to gobble up wanton assets and twist around market prices. The impact of the screwy prices is to make a mockery of resource allocation in the financial forum as well as the real economy.

Despite the upsurge of the assets in play, no groundswell can keep growing forever. The inevitable outcome is a bombshell that has to burst at some point.

The greater the buildup, the bigger is the bang when it finally does occur. If the blowup is large enough, the entire system of finance and economics comes tumbling down in one unholy mess.

Securing the Future

It may sound like an exaggeration to say that a single outfit or a small crew of actors could slash gaping holes in the fabric of civilization. Yet the debacle of 2008, along with its fallout, has given us a spine-tingling preview of what lies in store. On current trends, a catastrophe that nukes the trappings of modernity is not only possible but inevitable.

If the economy falls apart, then the security of the global society hangs in the balance. In the 20th century, the Great Depression provided the breeding ground for the poverty, misery and aggression that gave rise to the Second World War.

There is no reason to suppose that a similar fate – even worse – can be avoided in the future. A sweeping blowup of the global system of finance and trade, along with implosion of the economy round the world, would set the stage for a repeat performance.

The next time around, though, a big difference will lie in the vast stockpiles of weapons of mass destruction. The armaments of this strain range from nuclear missiles to biological munitions. Things could get ugly real quick.

In the popular imagination, the destruction of our way of life will come about – if it does at all – through an act of god from the heavens above. A case in point is a killer asteroid that upends the planet and throws our kind back to the Stone Age.

As it happens, though, we are quite capable of wreaking mayhem on a comparable scale with our own hands. Moreover, a blowup of such magnitude is more likely to be sparked by arms of financial leverage than weapons of physical violence. If we leave things the way they are, we will surely meet that gruesome fate sooner or later.

On the bright side, though, we could stave off the advent of doomsday by a mere act of forethought along with the legislation to match. The apt course of action would be plain, quick and sound.

On the other hand, the roundup of regulation will be far from easy to accomplish due to the mass of opposition from the vested interests along with their lobbying organs. In this grungy setting, the staunch course of action will require the fortitude of the statesmen in office along with the backing of their constituents.

On a positive note, though, it would take only a small fraction of the voting public, numbering in the millions, to see the project through. The stalwarts would be acting on behalf of the entire population of consumers and producers that count in the billions across the planet.

It's a truism that many things in life are knotty and complex. Yet, there are rare cases in which the proper course of action comes into plain view. Moreover, the best tack happens to be free of noxious byproducts. All that is needed is the pluck to do the right thing.

The blowup of 2008 has shown that extreme levels of leverage can bring down the entire edifice of finance and economics. Whether the assailants happen to be hedge funds or other hounds bulked up by leverage, it would make sense to defang the agents of armageddon.

Moreover, it would be helpful to take the proper measures before the bell tolls for all in the financial ring as well as the real economy. As much as we may wish, whistling in the dark will not rid the world of the specter of meltdown.

Wrapping Up

Hedge funds come in all shapes, stripes and scales. On the spectrum of bulk, the gnats at the low end of the range can barely muster a few thousand dollars or a couple of million bucks.

At the opposite end of the spectrum dwell the hulks, each of which can throw around a war chest amounting to billions of dollars. The punters of this breed include veiled outfits acting on their own as well as sheltered groups ensconced within commercial banks, insurance companies, and the like.

The swarm of hedge funds exhibits a great deal of diversity in terms of trading styles, market niches, and so on. Even so, the entire throng of punters shares one common trait at least.

The universal streak is the urge to make a fast buck. In fact, the lure of quick wealth lies at the heart of the sales pitch to prospective clients.

In a mad rush to hit the jackpot in a jiffy, the operators take on scads of risk far beyond the bounds of prudence. The dangers of the risky moves are often compounded by the uptake of leverage.

In this context, the schemes employed take the form of loans from external parties or tools of hideous strength. Needless to say, the impact of levered ploys is to magnify the threats even further.

Not surprisingly, hedge funds of all stripes blow up in droves whether the economy happens to be surging or slumping. To make matters worse for the investing public, the usual statistics bandied about in the marketplace serve to cover up the reality of tatty performance by the hedgies.

On a positive note, though, a string of serious studies has begun to reveal the extent of the damage that the hapless clients have endured for decades on end. The punch line is that the patrons in the aggregate get a raw deal in the hedge fund game.

On top of it all, the throng of hedge funds poses a serious threat to the real economy along with the global system of finance and trade. Given this backdrop, it makes no sense to leave the financial security of an entire nation, much less the whole planet, in thrall to a bogey of such magnitude.

To let the danger mount would be foolhardy in the extreme. On the upside, though, the bugbear could be defanged in one fell swoop.

All that is required is a stroke of deft legislation, along with the fortitude of civic leaders and the support of beleaguered citizens. As we have seen in this book, it's not only the throng of investors that would benefit from the abolition of runaway speculation. Rather, the entire population of consumers and producers round the world would be saved from the menace.

Each person, each outfit, each nation, has a stake in stamping out the specter of total breakdown. It's hard to imagine anything in the global economy that deserves more attention without further delay.

Moving Forward

As a matter of public policy, elected officials should not play chicken with the financial system. The standard practice of the government is to wait until it's nearly too late to save the day. Under the conventional scheme, it's only a matter of time before the whole shebang comes tumbling down with a real bang.

In a number of niches, the public sector has a habit of stepping in to harness the penchant for gambling by the general public. In the case of a lottery, for instance, the government may intervene by taking over the operation in its entirety.

The authorities tend to get involved even when a bounded form of gambling poses no threat at all to the community at large. As an example, a lottery or a casino has no impact on the robustness of the capital markets or the vitality of the entire economy. Even so, the government keeps a watchful eye on the goings-on by way of licensing, ownership or other means.

To an increasing degree, the swarm of hedge funds has played a starring role in causing or exacerbating the blowups in the marketplace. A thoughtful observer would find it difficult to refute the role of hedge funds as agents of mass destruction.

In this milieu, the way forward is clear. The only real question is whether there is enough gumption among elected officials to step up to the challenge and seize the fiend by the horns.

The alternative is also plain enough. Under the current system of wanton risk and unchecked leverage, it's only a matter of time before the army of hedge funds does some serious damage to the global system of finance and commerce.

In that case, the carnage will go far beyond the wipeout of a few trillion dollars here and there. It might sound like an exaggeration, but the truth is that we ain't seen nuttin' yet.

The custom of the past was to putter on the sidelines and slap on a few bandages here and there. But experience has shown that puttering round the issues with a piecemeal approach will not fill the bill.

To round up, it would be a good idea to deal with the threat while we still have the chance. Otherwise everyone in the global economy is destined to pay dearly for the lack of forethought and initiative.

If things continue the way they are, then we won't have to wait for a visitation from the heavens above to stamp out our way of life. Rather, we on Earth will have the privilege of bringing on doomsday on our own.

Hedge funds of all breeds, be they midget organs or mammoth creatures, have easy access to arms of monstrous leverage as well as weapons of mass carnage. In the natural flow of events, it's only a matter of time before the free play of unchecked risk leads to untold grief.

Looking at the larger picture, the financial forum as a whole is a treacherous place teeming with sham data and groundless rumor, tricky guile and false hope. In this slippery landscape, the worldly investor has to reach beyond the illusion of performance and take in the reality of adversity.

Things are not always what they seem at first sight. For this reason, a primal task of the earnest investor is to glean the wheat from the chaff, the fact from the myth.

A sturdy grasp of the marketplace paves the way for a lucid approach to minding a personal portfolio. The same is true in fixing up a trenchant program of public policy in order to ensure the stabilty of the financial markets and the security of the larger society.

Annex A

Beacon beyond the Murk

In an effort to boost their returns from investing, a lot of punters dart in and out of the market in quick succession. Whether the eager beavers happen to be full-time professionals or part-time amateurs, the lure of quick profits is just too tempting to ignore.

On the whole, though, the frenetic efforts of the gamers all but come to naught. In fact, the final outcome is usually worse than zilch. Despite the huge toll in terms of time and money plus toil and sweat, the mass of schemes meant to outrun the market end up achieving precisely the opposite.

The sad state of affairs is spotlighted by the average performance of mutual funds, which have an uncanny knack of lagging the benchmarks of the stock market. Meanwhile, the outturn for individual investors is sadder still: in the zany world of finance, the average investor lags the market averages by a sizable margin.

But the story does not end there, for a bigger jolt awaits. The worst showing in the arena is turned in by the pros who flaunt the image of being the best and the brightest of the lot; namely the throng of operators in the hedge fund game.

Slow Lane Beats the Fast Track

On one hand, the usual statistics purport to show that the gross returns of the hedgies are comparable to those of the market at large – or perhaps even better. In reality, though, the gamesters as a group manage to lose gobs of money when the results are adjusted for errors due to biased sampling.

Since the gross returns of hedge funds are negative, the net payoff for their customers is of course even worse. The additional takedown stems from burden of administrative costs such as performance fees and maintenance charges.

The cruddy returns of the wildcats is spotlighted by the top tier of hedge funds; namely, the heavyweights whose records are open to public view. As a group, the best of the breed turns in a shabby showing that trails far behind the average returns of the investing public. In fact, the performance of the behemoths is so abysmal that they die off at the rate of nearly one-half every couple of years.

The main reason for the rubout springs from a manic urge to take on risky bets in the hope of hitting home runs. Unfortunately, the dicey gambits end up backfiring in due course. The upshot is to hammer the portfolios and clobber the patrons, whether in the form of investors or creditors.

Despite the barrage of grim news, there is a glint of sunshine in the world of investing. Mindful players who pursue a guarded approach to investing can beat the market for years or even decades on end.

The real champions with staying power are the ones that veer away from flimsy schemes to get rich quick. In fact, the path to success lies in the opposite direction.

The way to prevail over the long range is to pursue a thoughtful strategy rather than an impulsive one. The trusty course favors durable trends over fleeting fads, cautious plays over iffy ploys, sedate investing over frantic trading.

Leading Light in the Forum

The most respected name in the financial world is a demure investor rather than an antsy speculator: Warren Buffett of Omaha, Nebraska. Since the 1960s, the wizard has turned his investment vehicle, Berkshire Hathaway, into a powerhouse on Wall Street.

The holding company takes up sizable stakes in operating firms that appeal to Buffett's penchant for value. The maestro picks out companies that are undervalued, then acquires large blocks of equity to have and to hold for the long haul. To safeguard the hefty stake in a chosen firm, Buffett is wont to join the board of directors and help to shepherd the business to greater heights.

Survival of the Sober

Thanks to the farsighted approach, the shareholders of Berkshire Hathaway have enjoyed outsize returns over investment horizons of varied lengths. A case in point is the solid performance shown around the turn of the millennium.

As a point of reference, a share of class A stock in Berkshire was worth $8,350 at the beginning of 1990. By the end of 2007, the equity reached a high of $151,650 per share. The average gain over that period came out to some 17.5% per year.

Amid the collapse of the stock market in October 2008, the equity tumbled to a low of $105,300. Unlike many other players in the arena, though, the juggernaut was in no danger of going bankrupt in short order.

Given the blowout in the financial sector and the real economy, many of the largest firms found themselves in dire straits. As an example, a clutch of giants in the financial sector teetered on the brink of bankruptcy while a bunch of their peers actually tumbled over the edge.

Without a helping hand from the government, a slew of firms on Wall Street as well as Main Street would have gone the way of the dodo. Among the basket cases rescued by the public sector were American icons such as General Motors and Goldman Sachs.

Whomping the Competition

Given the broad reach across multiple sectors of the economy, Berkshire Hathaway could not help but slump to some extent in the throes of the financial crisis. Throughout the ordeal, however, the company was an island of calm compared to the bedlam of the market at large.

In 2008, the price of Berkshire stock fell by 9.6% at a time when the Standard & Poor's 500 index plunged by 37%. During the year to follow, the staunch equity rose by 19.8% while the market benchmark climbed by 26.5%.

Despite the inevitable setbacks from time to time, Berkshire has a habit of outpacing the market benchmarks as well as managed accounts such as mutual funds. In particular, the dynamo rose by 22% per year on average over the prolonged stretch ranging from 1965 to 2009.

A return on investment at that pace adds up to a princely sum over the course of the decades. The best way to appreciate the fruits of lusty growth is to look at a telling example.

Suppose that an investor had committed $10,000 to Berkshire in October 1964, then sat back and watched from the sidelines for 45 years. In that case, the nest egg would have ballooned to $80 million by the end of 2009. To account for inflation, however, we should note that the original stake was worth some $60,000 in contemporary dollars.

By way of comparison, we can examine the performance of the top pair of spearheads in the mutual fund industry. If the same amount of capital had been committed at the outset, then a position in the Fidelity Magellan Fund would have grown to roughly $9.1 million over the same period. Meanwhile the corresponding figure for the Templeton Growth Fund would be about $2.9 million.

On the other hand, the market as a whole would not have fared anywhere near as well. In particular, the S&P index clambered by 9.3% per year on average over this stretch. As a result, a pot of $10,000 at the outset would have turned into a pile worth close to $560,000 by the end.[42]

To round up, Berkshire was able to trounce the aces in the land of mutual funds. Meanwhile, the lead over the market as a whole was a lot bigger.

After adjusting for errors due to biased sampling, hedge funds are known to trail far behind mutual funds. For this reason, there's scarcely any point in comparing the performance of Berkshire against the plight of the wildcats.

In fact, any attempt to compare the two approaches – prudent investing versus manic trading – would be largely hypothetical. The reason is that hedge funds have a way of dying off like mayflies whether the conditions in the marketplace happen to be benign or malign.

As noted earlier, the half-life of a hedge fund is hardly more than a couple of years. For this reason, an observer would be hard-pressed to find a hedgie that could even survive the lengthy span covering nearly half a century, let alone flourish over the interval.

In that case, the amount of profits – or lack of such – would be beside the point. For want of a challenger, Berkshire would have to be declared the winner by default.

Mirage of the Hedge Fund Game

The vale of hedge funds is not the land of milk and honey that it's usually made out to be. Rather, the mass of wildcats take up unsound bets in the vain hope of hitting the jackpot.

This treacherous domain swallows up a horde of hopefuls that show up and try out their luck. But the gamesters quickly fritter away their chips, fall by the wayside, and fade into the night. As the duds depart from the scene, they take along whatever booty they managed to snatch up while the tryout was in progress.

In a way, the plungers do achieve their aim of making a killing: the bulk of players lunge out, hang themselves, and die off like lemmings. In the process, the eager beavers grind down the money entrusted to them and leave their patrons in the lurch.

In the tumultuous history of hedge funds, the Quantum Fund was arguably the most celebrated name in the field. As we saw in Chapter 6, however, even the goliath ended up falling on its sword and biting the dust just like the mass of punters in the arena.

Despite the generic traits, however, there are of course certain features – however wispy or fleeting – that distinguish the achiever from the wannabe in the hedge fund game. Pretty much by definition, a pacesetter can turn in a respectable profit for a prolonged spell which could last for years at a time.

On the other hand, the extent to which the payoff can be ascribed to financial acumen rather than sheer luck is entirely debatable. Whatever the performance to date, the specter of a blowup is an ever-present threat for the leader in the field as well as the rank and file.

Given the twisted pattern of incentives for the operators, a great deal of self-control is needed to rein in the impulse to take on gross amounts of risk. In fact, the key to survival is the grit to keep the venal urge in check. Depending on the degree of restraint, a particular outfit could end up lasting longer or shorter than the rest of the pack.

Moving Ahead by Holding Back

The financial ring is a topsy-turvy place where seasoned professionals often trail behind rank amateurs. Given the wacky nature of the marketplace, the earnest investor would do well to take a skeptical approach to any fanciful schemes for making a fast buck.

An exemplar involves the hullabaloo over the sizzling returns that hedge funds are said to achieve. In this corner of the bazaar, the illusion of profits is maintained by a slipshod tally of data that is entirely at odds with the underlying truth. More precisely, a simple-minded mash-up of hand-picked cases can churn out statistics which match or even surpass the performance of the market benchmarks.

After taking into account the flaws in sampling, however, hedge funds as a group lag far behind the yardsticks of the market. In fact, the gamers are notable for the exceptional ability to destroy wealth while dabbling in a market whose long-term trend happens to be upward.

The true state of affairs in the hedge fund game is masked by the sleight of hand involved in compiling the data and crunching the numbers. In any field of inquiry, *a cherry-picked subset drawn solely from the current crop of survivors cannot be taken at face value in assessing the lot of the population.*

On a positive note, the news from the circus of finance is not entirely dismal. Amid the muddle and the mayhem, there are occasional streaks of light and hope.

A showcase lies in the value of a passive approach. In general, glitzy schemes for beating the market benchmarks may sound appealing at first glance but in fact fail to deliver the goods. Instead, the vast majority of investors could improve their score by a hefty amount if they embraced a slow and steady approach.

For this purpose, a wise tack is to invest in index funds whose mission is to track the benchmarks of the market. An investor who can pretty much keep up with the yardsticks will perform far better than the bulk of their peers. The punters in the latter category include full-time pros as well as part-time tyros.

In short, the simplest and quickest way for the mass of investors to uplift their return on investment is to turn away from flaky schemes for beating the market averages. Instead, a turnout in close range of the benchmarks would place the wily players in a league of their own.

To some folks, the goal of tracking the market averages may seem like the recourse of a defeatist. Based on the reality of the marketplace, however, the objective should not be viewed in a pessimistic light. Rather, the policy is in fact a trenchant way for most investors to boost their return on investment by a sizable amount.

The sworn enemies of the investor are the demons of greed and fear. The ghouls show up most often, and inflict the most damage, in the throes of a roily market on an upswing or a downstroke.

In addition, the investor should keep in mind that the prospects for upgrowth as well as wipeout differ from one industry to another, and even from one company to the next. As an example, the firms in the technology sector or the emerging markets face a choppier environment compared to their brethren involved with consumer staples or developed countries. Due to the heightened risk, the equities in the dynamic niches of the marketplace tend to be more volatile than the others.

Unfortunately, the wild swings in price have a way of throwing the investors for a loop. The plight of the battered players is hightlighted by their performance in dealing with index funds.

The purpose of an index fund is to track the returns on a benchmark of the market. In that case, the customers of the pool should in principle be able turn in a showing comparable to that of the yardstick itself. Sadly, though, the practice differs grossly from the theory.

Volatility Spoils Self-Control and Payoff

A leading light in the realm of index funds is found in John Bogle, founder of the Vanguard Group of investment vehicles. The patriarch examined the returns of 79 index funds in a number of categories over a period of five years ending in 2009. Each of the investment pools was structured as an *exchange traded fund* (ETF) whose shares could be bought and sold by the investing public just like any other equity in the stock market.

According to the probe, the investors lagged the performance of the index funds across the board. The best showing – meaning the least underperformance – occurred for the funds that take a value-oriented approach to investing in large companies.

Serene Cruise

For the latter class of funds, the average return on investment was minus 1.8% per year. Meanwhile, the corresponding figure for the customers of the same pools was negative 2.2%. In other words, the investors trailed behind the average ETF in this category by a small gap of 0.4% per annum.

The funds which take a value-oriented approach to investing offer a sedate ride compared to their peers aiming for fast growth. For this reason, we would expect a lot of the customers to stay put rather than jump ship during the upswings and downlegs in the marketplace.

In that case, the clients as a group would have scant reason to lag the vessels themselves. The logic is in fact borne out by the data.

Of the nine funds included in this category, the clientele was able to keep up with the investment pool in nearly half the cases. From the opposite stance, the customers trailed behind the fund in five of the nine cases.

Modest Tossing

The equities of midsize firms straddle the middle range between the extremes of volatility. Due to the turbulence, we would expect the investing public to fare worse with mid-cap stocks than with their larger siblings.

The study included five funds which focused on a blend of mid-cap stocks. For each of these vehicles, the customers trailed behind the ETF itself.

Within this cluster, the average gain eked out by the funds was positive 0.4% a year. By contrast, the mean return for the investors was negative 3.0%. In other words, the patrons lagged the funds by 3.4% per annum on average.

Rough Ride

At the far end of the scale, the worst performance cropped up for the pools in the financial sector. For this category, the average return for the funds was negative 10.7% a year. By contrast, the mean performance of the investing public was minus 28.6% per annum. Based on the last two figures, the underperformance of the investors was negative 17.9% a year on average.

The second worst category lay in emerging markets. For this breed of ETF vehicles, the average pool was able to bag a profit of 15.6% a year. On the other hand, the investing public managed to turn in only 3.8%. In other words, the investors trailed behind the index funds by 11.8% a year on average.

Not surprisingly, the trouncing of the clients was unanimous for the roughest rides. Of the five funds dealing with the financial sector, the customers trailed behind the vehicle in every case. The story was similar for the three vessels focused on emerging markets.[43]

Normal versus Oddball

At this stage, we ought to note a couple of routine as well as exceptional features of the results presented above. The generic aspect lies in the fact that the size of the lag by investors was tied largely to the volatility of the market.

The rougher the ride, the greater was the underperformance. The reason, of course, is that investors have a habit of dashing in and out of the market at precisely the wrong times.

The gamers pile into the bazaar in the throes of a bubble when they should be running away; and they flee in droves in the depths of a crash when they ought to be jumping in with both feet.

The unusual outcome of the foregoing study lay in the yucky performance of the investors in the financial sector. As a rule, the stocks in this corner of the market tend to be more sedate than average.

On the other hand, the financial crisis of 2008 dealt a heavy blow to commercial banks, insurance firms, and the like during and after the fiasco. As a result, the stocks in this sector thrashed more violently than the marke as a whole. Due to the extreme levels of volatility, the investors fell into hysterics and thereby lost more money than usual.

From a longer perspective, the most volatile niches of the stock market are to be found in emerging markets, technology ventures, and small companies. By contrast, the most stable segments include large firms, utility companies, health care, and the like.

In spite of the differences, though, one common thread runs throughout the marketplace. The higher the volatility, the greater is the underperformance of the investor.

The results of the study underscore the fact that most investors would enjoy a big increase in earnings if they stopped meddling with their portfolios. The best course of action is to adopt a farsighted strategy and ignore the goings-on in the bazaar in the interim.

Unfortunately, self-control is in short supply in the orgy of finance. Instead, the mass of participants has a way of darting in and out of the market at exactly the wrong times.

The greater the turbulence, the bigger is the lag of the investor behind the target benchmark. To guard against the folly, the best thing that the vast majority of players can do for themselves is to follow a two-step procedure.

The first act is to set up a program of automatic investments into one or more index funds that track promising branches of the marketplace. Depending on the planning horizon, the niches of this stripe span the gamut from health care and digital technology to smallish firms and emerging countries.

The second – and far more difficult – task is to stick to the sedate agenda. The strategy should be refined and the portfolio updated according to a fixed schedule, perhaps once every year or so.

On the other hand, the antics of bourse over the short run should be ignored completely. In fact, the wisest course of action in many cases is to stay away from the financial bazaar for years or even decades on end.

For the bulk of investors, there's a simple way to uplift their performance. The trusty way to earn a lot more is to do a lot less. As a rule, the best course of action is inaction.

Flying High for Real

To round up, myriads of punters would increase their earnings by a hefty amount if they could just sit tight and stop fiddling with their assets. In that case, the ease of boosting profits without any effort to speak of happens to be a free lunch that begs to be snatched up.

While we're on the subject of gainful strategies, closing the gap between the actual and the potential is not the only hunk of juicy news. For the investor who wants to excel, another type of fruitful move awaits.

There are in fact a number of ways to outpace the market over the long haul. An obvious approach is to adopt the opposite tack of the average investor at each stage. The winning tactic is to move in when the general public abhors the market, and step out when the crowd adores it.

The problem with the foregoing technique, of course, is that it requires more grit than most people can muster. If the situation were otherwise, then the average investor would not be found lagging the market averages.

In addition, there are certain methods which are somewhat less demanding on the investor in terms of the discipline required. Moreover, many of the trenchant methods happen to be straightforward: the techniques entail just about nothing in the way of skill or effort, time or money. Rather, the toughest requirement on the investor is the fortitude to stick to the agenda.

As a caveat, though, none of the trusty tacks will enable the player to rake in gobs of money in a flash. The frightful performance of eager beavers such as hedge funds should make it clear that the punters in a rush are doomed to bite the dust in droves.

To sum up, a variety of methods can be used to outshine the benchmarks of the market over the long haul. Certain schemes can help the investor in boosting the expected gain, while others may trim the likely risk, and still others to accomplish a mix of both.

These are all fetching and rewarding topics for discussion. On the other hand, the main purpose of this book is to sort out the problems with hedge funds and to present the opportunities for thwarting the threats through a coherent set of policies.

For this reason, the nitty-gritty of molding a systematic program of investment lies beyond the scope of this volume. On a positive note, though, the armory of practical techniques and handy tools for minding a portfolio will be taken up by other guidebooks within the same series.

In the meantime, a number of related topics are discussed from sundry viewpoints in the collection of publications listed in the *References* section. A brief introduction to the resources is provided in Annex B.

Annex B

Pointers to Further Information

If the performance of managed funds is so dismal, then there must be better ways for a mindful investor to nurture a nest egg. Most of all, is there a *simple* approach for outpacing the mass of players including the army of mutual funds, hedge funds, and individual investors?

Remarkably, the answer is a resounding *Yes*. For instance, a plain strategy involves the use of one or more index funds whose role is to track the benchmarks of the market.

In recent years, a growing throng of investors has flocked to a type of vehicle known as the *exchange traded fund* (ETF). A key advantage for the customer lies in the ease of buying and selling the shares of an ETF through an equity account at a brokerage firm. Another attraction lies in the low level of maintenance fees.

Further information on this topic is available in an article titled "How to Beat the Investment Funds: Outrun Most Mutual Funds and Hedge Funds while Earning a Bonus" (Kim, 2011b). A link to the write-up is given in the following module on *References*.

The problems described in this book – ranging from hidden threats to lousy returns – are applicable to a host of investment vehicles. The vessels at risk span the gamut from communal funds to individual stocks.

In practice, though, the threat is greatest when the rate of mortality is high; or equivalently, the proportion of survivors is low. A paragon of course lies in the swarm of hedge funds.

Further information on the subject is available in a set of articles under the rubric of *Hedge Funds* (Kim, 2011a). An example within the collection is a write-up on the prospects for wildcat pools over the decades to come. A link to the suite of articles is given in the next segment of this book.

More generally, the compilation of resources in the *References* section covers a diverse selection of treats. The nuggets span the gamut from breezy articles published in general newspapers to weighty studies reported in academic journals.

References

Barr, A. "Simons, Griffin, Lampert Earn over $1 Bln in 2006." 2007/4/24. http://www.marketwatch.com/news/story/simons-griffin-lampert-earn-more/story.aspx?guid=%7B55DBE196-3461-495D-8B27-DE4CA6C5641D%7D – tapped 2010/7/13.

Bogle, J. C. "Index Funds in Mid-2009: A Status Report." Also titled as "Fireside Chat: A Discussion With John Bogle." 2009/6/17. http://www.indexuniverse.com/docs/BogleWebinar.pdf – tapped 2011/1/14.

Brown, S. J., W. N. Goetzmann, and J. Park. "Conditions for Survival: Changing Risk and the Performance of Hedge Fund Managers and CTAs." Stern School of Business, New York, 1999/6/30. http://www.stern.nyu.edu/fin/workpapers/papers99/wpa99077.pdf – tapped 2010/7/12.

Cassidy, J. "Hedge Clipping." 2007/07/02. http://www.newyorker.com/reporting/2007/07/02/070702fa_fact_cassidy?printable=true#ixzz0tk6j6g8j – tapped 2010/7/15.

Duhigg, C. "Stock Traders Find Speed Pays, in Milliseconds." 2009/7/23. http://www.nytimes.com/2009/07/24/business/24trading.html?_r=1 – tapped 2010/7/27.

Economist, The. "Time to Rebalance". 2010a/4/3, Special Report, pp. 3-5. Also at http://www.economist.com/node/15793036 – tapped 2011/1/12.

Economist, The. "High-Frequency Traders: Spread Betting." 2010b/8/14, pp. 56-57. Also at http://www.economist.com/node/16792950 – tapped 2011/1/12.

Fatality Analysis Reporting System. "National Statistics". Undated. http://www-fars.nhtsa.dot.gov/Main/index.aspx – tapped 2010/7/31.

Fung, W. K. H., and D. A. Hsieh. "Hedge Funds: An Industry in Its Adolescence". *Economic Review,* FRB Atlanta, v. 91(4), 2006, pp. 1-34. http://www.frbatlanta.org/filelegacydocs/erq406_fung.pdf – tapped 2010/7/11.

Goetzmann, W. N., J. Ingersoll Jr., and S. A. Ross. High-Water Marks and Hedge Fund Management Contracts. Yale School of Management, New Haven, 2001/4/18. http://icf.som.yale.edu/working_papers/papers/2001/Goetzmann04A.pdf – tapped 2010/7/12.

Griffin, J. M., and J. Xu. "How Smart are the Smart Guys? A Unique View from Hedge Fund Stock Holdings". Working Paper, Univ. of Texas at Austin, 2009; *Review of Financial Studies*, v. 22(7), 2009, pp. 2531-2570; doi:10.1093/rfs/hhp026. Also at http://www.jgriffin.info/Research/RFSJuly1108.pdf – tapped 2009/9/3.

International Herald Tribune. "Insider Trading Conviction of Soros is Upheld." 2006/06/14. http://www.nytimes.com/2006/06/14/business/worldbusiness/14iht-soros.1974397.html – tapped 2011/1/14.

Karchmer, J. "A Shakeup at Soros Funds." April 28, 2000. http://money.cnn.com/2000/04/28/mutualfunds/soros – tapped 2010/7/13.

Kim, S. *Hedge Funds*. Suite at Knol. http://knol.google.com/k/steven-kim/hedge-funds/30p6914355voj/9# – tapped 2011a/2/6.

Kim, S. "How to Beat the Investment Funds: Outrun Most Mutual Funds and Hedge Funds while Earning a Bonus". http://www.mintkit.com/beat-investment-funds – tapped 2011b/2/8.

Malkiel, B. G., and A. Saha. "Hedge Funds: Risk and Return". *Financial Analysts Journal*, Vol. 61, No. 6, pp. 80-88, 2005. Also at http://www.cfapubs.org/doi/pdf/10.2469/faj.v61.n6.2775.

Mamudi, S. "Beaten by Buffett: Mutual Funds Dramatically Lag Berkshire Stock during Chairman's Tenure." 2010/3/5. http://www.marketwatch.com/story/buffett-and-berkshire-outperform-all-mutual-funds-2010-03-05?pagenumber=2 – tapped 2010/7/20.

Market Folly. "Renaissance Technologies' Medallion Fund: Performance Numbers Illustrated." 2010/6/9. http://www.marketfolly.com/2010/06/renaissance-technologies-medallion-fund.html – tapped 2010/7/17.

Max, K. "Multibillionaire Speculator Soros Exiting Risk Business." TheStreet.com, 2000/4/28. http://www.thestreet.com/story/929295/multibillionaire-speculator-soros-exiting-risk-business.html – tapped 2010/7/13.

Morgenson, G. "Soros's Quantum Fund Losses in Russia Put at $2 Billion." 1998/8/27. http://www.nytimes.com/1998/08/27/business/international-business-soros-s-quantum-fund-losses-in-russia-put-at-2-billion.html – tapped 2010/7/15.

Norris, F. "French Court upholds Soros Conviction." 2005/3/25. http://www.nytimes.com/2005/03/24/business/worldbusiness/24iht-soros.html?_r=1 – tapped 2011/1/14.

Patterson, S., and J. Strasburg. "Pioneering Fund Stages Second Act." 2010/3/16. http://online.wsj.com/article/SB10001424052748703494404575082000779302566.html – tapped 2010/7/14.

Posthuma, N., and P. J. van der Sluis. "A Reality Check on Hedge Fund Returns". Free University Amsterdam, and ABP Investments. Working Memo, July 2003. http://dare.ubvu.vu.nl/bitstream/1871/10239/1/20030017.pdf – tapped 2010/7/11.

Renaissance Technologies. "About Renaissance." https://www.renfund.com/vm/index.vm – tapped 2011/2/1.

Son, H. "AIG's Trustees Shun 'Shadow Board,' Seek Directors (Update2)".

http://www.bloomberg.com/apps/news?pid=20601103&sid=aaog3i4yU
opo&refer=us – tapped 2009/12/6.

Spiro, L. N., and S. Woolley. "Long-Term Capital Management: What
You Need to Know". *BusinessWeek*, 1998/10/12.
http://www.businessweek.com/archives/1998/b3599077.arc.htm –
tapped 2010/7/11.

Tagliabue, J. "Soros Is Found Guilty in France On Charges of Insider
Trading." 2002/12/21.
http://www.nytimes.com/2002/12/21/business/soros-is-found-guilty-in-
france-on-charges-of-insider-trading.html – tapped 2010/7/17.

Teitelbaum, R. "Simons at Renaissance Cracks Code, Doubling Assets
(Update1)." 2007/11/27.
http://www.bloomberg.com/apps/news?pid=newsarchive&sid=aq33M3
X795vQ – tapped 2010/7/17.

Teitelbaum, R., and K. Burton. "Ex-Simons Employees Say Firm
Pursued Illegal Trades (Correct)." 2007/7/30.
http://www.bloomberg.com/apps/news?pid=newsarchive&sid=agxVXC
.r9Edw – tapped 2010/7/18.

Vickers, M. "$5 Billion Hedge Fund Gets Clipped." 2005/12/2.
http://money.cnn.com/2005/12/01/markets/englander_fortune/index.ht
m?section=money_topstories – tapped 2010/7/18.

Wall Street Journal. "Top 100 Hedge Funds." Undated.
http://s.wsj.net/public/resources/documents/TOP100-HEDGE-FUNDS-
BA-100524.pdf – tapped 2010/7/15.

Wikipedia. "Lottery". http://en.wikipedia.org/wiki/Lottery – tapped
2011/1/12.

World Federation of Exchanges. "Key Market Figures." June 2010.
http://www.world-exchanges.org/statistics/key-market-figures – tapped
2010/7/2.

Notes

[1] Goetzmann et al., 2001.

[2] Brown et al., 1999.

[3] Fatality, 2010.

[4] We will consider an outcome to be a success if the portfolio at hand beats a standard benchmark such as the S&P 500 index. Meanwhile, the opposite turnout is regarded as a failure.

There is of course a negligible chance that the performance of the account and the index will be identical. Then the outcome can be considered a draw. In that case, the simplest course of action is to ignore the result and to replace it with another trial.

For our example, the probability of success equals one-half; and likewise the chance of failure. Since the odds of a failure for the stocks are independent, the chance that each of the 5 accounts ends up as a loser is ½ to the fifth power.

The latter expression can be written more tersely as $(1/2)^5$. After crunching the numbers, the resulting value comes out to a mite over 0.03. Put another way, the probability that all 5 pools turn out to be losers happens to be about 3 percent.

In that case, the complementary value of some 97 percent is the chance that at least one of the pools is successful. In other words, the prospect of trumping the market index with one or more portfolios is around 97 percent.

[5] As a starting point for discussion, we said that 97 percent is the chance that at least one out of the five accounts set up at the outset turns out to be a winner. In other words, the prospect of trumping the market index with one or more portfolios is about 97 percent.

The latter figure is actually an extremely conservative estimate of the chance of success. In practice, the odds of producing a winner are much higher. The reason has to do with the difference between large and small firms listed in the stock market.

In general, the number of stocks traded on the bourse is prone to vary from one day to the next. For one thing, tired firms drop out of the stock market entirely while fresh concerns step into the ring for the first time.

Despite the fluctuation in numbers over time, the U.S. market contains roughly a myriad stocks; that is, around 10,000 securities. Among the companies listed on an exchange, the S&P benchmark contains 500 of the biggest names. In other words, roughly 1 in 20 stocks on the bourse belongs to the roster of giants tracked by the index. For our purpose here, the rest of the crowd may be viewed as the small fry.

At this stage, we should note that the small firms listed on the stock market tend to grow faster than the big ones. As a result, the equities of the minnows are prone to outpace those of the whales.

The superior performance of the shrimps as a whole tends to show up clearly over the course of a multiyear wave in the stock market. The undulation of the bourse is tied to the business cycle in the real economy, which usually crops up a couple of times over the course of a decade.

Given the prevalence of small firms in the marketplace, a stock picked at random is likely to belong to a shrimp rather than a whale with a probability of 500 out of 10,000. The latter ratio is of course equivalent to 1 out of 20.

From the opposite stance, the likelihood of selecting a lightweight turns out to be 19 out of 20. Put another way, the chance of picking a minnow in a blind draw is apt to be 95%.

To keep things simple, let's assume that 95% is in fact the precise chance that a stock picked willy-nilly will end up trumping the S&P index. In the converse direction, the prospect of lagging the benchmark comes out to 5%.

What's the likelihood that 5 stocks picked at random will all lag the market index? This crummy event will occur with a probability of 1/20 to the fifth power; that is, $(1/20)^5$. The resulting expression is equal to 1 out of 3,200,000.

When written as a decimal, the latter value comes out to a tad over 0.0000003. In other words, the chance of ending up with 5 losers is far less than a thousandth of 1 percent.

The complement of the preceding fraction is the probability that at least one of the stocks turns out to be a winner. Put another way, the chance of creating at least one portfolio that beats the market index is well over 99.9999 percent.

Granted, we could quibble over one aspect of the analysis: whether the chance of a wanton stock beating the market benchmark happens to be exactly 95% or some other value. On the other hand, a couple of factors turn this matter into a non-issue.

For one thing, all that is required to improve the probability of success is to increase the number of stocks in each portfolio. As an extreme example, an account that replicates the performance of a benchmark for small firms will almost surely beat the S&P 500 index. The same is true for a pool of midsize stocks. The superior outcome is apt to ensue especially over the course of a business cycle that lasts around half a decade or so.

A second factor lies in the robustness of the argument in the face of minor variations in the prospects of success for a single stock picked at random. In other words, no reasonable tweaking of the probability will affect the final conclusion regarding the ease of concocting a winning portfolio.

To wrap up, picking 5 stocks at random will virtually ensure that at least one of the choices ends up as a winner. The moral of the story: fabricating a track record in the stock market is far, far easier than most people believe.

[6] Posthuma and van der Sluis, 2003.
[7] Posthuma and van der Sluis, 2003.
[8] Malkiel and Saha, 2005.
[9] Griffin and Xu, 2009.
[10] Fung and Hsieh, 2006.
[11] Griffin and Xu, 2009.
[12] Barr, 2007.
[13] Morgenson, 1998.
[14] Max, 2000.
[15] Karchmer, 2000.
[16] Tagliabue, 2002.
[17] *International*, 2006.
[18] Tagliabue, 2002.
[19] *International*, 2006.
[20] Norris, 2005.
[21] Barr, 2007.
[22] Cassidy, 2007.
[23] Teitelbaum, 2007.
[24] Teitelbaum, 2007.
[25] Renaissance, 2010.

[26] Teitelbaum and Burton, 2007.

[27] Vickers, 2005.

[28] *Wall*, 2010.

[29] Patterson and Strasburg, 2010.

[30] *Market*, 2010.

[31] Max, 2000.

[32] Mamudi, 2010.

[33] Duhigg, 2009.

[34] Duhigg, 2009.

[35] *Economist*, 2010b.

[36] World, 2010.

[37] As we noted earlier, the consumer surplus for a given market depends on the quantity demanded at each price level. The reader of an introductory textbook on economics will be aware that the surplus enjoyed by the buyers is defined by the enclosed area under the demand curve which also happens to lie above the price line. In a similar way, the area below the price line and above the supply curve corresponds to the seller surplus (Wikipedia, 2010).

In an attack of the scalpers during an uptrend in the market, the hoisted price is higher than the initial value. For this reason, the enclosed area above the price line has shrunk. Put another way, the buyer surplus has shriveled.

The ratio of the areas before and after the price change represents the fraction of the surplus retained by the buyers within the investing public. This proportion depends on a variety of factors. An example of the latter involves the specific values of the price level before and after the hike in price.

Another factor is the shape of the demand curve. For instance, an arc which is convex as seen from below is apt to result in a smaller loss in absolute dollars than the case of a straight slope.

On the other hand, the loss will be bigger in comparison to the total amount available at the outset, prior to the price hike. In other words, the relative loss for the investing public will be greater in the convex case than the drubbing due to a similar hike in price when the demand curve happens to be linear.

The pattern of abuse is reversed when the demand curve is concave. In that case, the cutout in terms of absolute dollars will be greater than the damage caused by a similar jack-up in price for the linear situation. However, the fractional loss – compared to the original amount of economic surplus – will be smaller.

Turning to a different but related issue, a second mode of loss stems from an abrupt distortion in the supply of shares. In particular, the relevant portion of the supply curve – namely, the section lying below the inflated price – is yanked to the left after the raiders scrounge up the equities lying below the threshold.

The outcome is a supply curve which has been broken into two pieces. One segment, lying above the newfound price, stands where it used to be before the raid by the scalpers. By contrast, the lower portion of the curve has been torn off and pushed leftward, closer to the vertical axis.

The raiders manage to snatch up the assets before the investors have a chance to learn that the information they possess is no longer relevant. More precisely, the initial level which they believe to be the current price is in fact outdated. When the shareowners give up their holdings at bargain prices, the seller surplus is lower than otherwise.

Part of the economic surfeit given up by the sellers is seized by the pirates that end up reselling the assets at higher prices. Another portion is lost entirely from the marketplace. The loss due to the offensive is reflected in the breakage of the supply curve along with the leftward shift of the lower segment of the arc.

In these ways, the economic surplus for the buyers as well sellers is crushed by the actions of the scalpers. Part of the surfeit lost by the sellers is swiped by the raiders, while the rest disappears completely from the marketplace.

To sum up, the attack of the bandits ends up yanking the pertinent portion of the supply curve to the left. The mangling of the arc is accompanied by a hike in the price level. The net impact is to squelch the overall trove of economic surplus available to the buyers as well as the sellers in the investment community.

How is it that the raiders are able to swipe so much of the economic surplus from the rest of the population? Isn't a free market supposed to be a fair forum where no one has any special advantage?

From a larger stance, the deficiency in the workings of the market springs from the shortage of timely information available to the investing public. In the throes of a blitzkrieg, ordinary investors are unable to grasp the true state of affairs.

When pandemonium breaks out, the shortfall of dope includes the latest value of the price signal. From the standpoint of expert traders, the blackout of information also includes a medley of additional cues such as the volume of transactions, or the rate of change in price for the asset in play.

As a result of the bushwhack, part of the economic surplus is transferred from the investors to the scalpers while another portion vanishes entirely from the marketplace. The upshot is a rubout of well-being for the entire population.

[38] Wikipedia, 2009.

[39] *Economist*, 2010a.

[40] Son, 2009.

[41] Spiro and Woolley, 1998.

[42] Mamudi, 2010.

[43] Bogle, 2009.

www.ingramcontent.com/pod-product-compliance
Lightning Source LLC
Chambersburg PA
CBHW072032190526
45165CB00017B/362